SAMS

Teach Yourself
Today

e-Baseball

SAMS Teach Yourself Today

e-Baseball

Mining the Internet for history, stats, fantasy leagues, and memorabilia

Bob Temple
with Introduction and Notes
by Rob Neyer

SAMS

201 West 103rd Street, Indianapolis, Indiana 46290

Sams Teach Yourself e-Baseball Today

Copyright © 2000 by Sams Publishing

International Standard Book Number: 0-672-31913-6

Printed in the United States of America

First Printing: March 2000

02   01   00   4   3   2   1

Trademarks

Warning and Disclaimer

Acquisitions Editors
Betsy Brown
Jeff Schultz

Development Editor
Damon Jordan

Managing Editor
Charlotte Clapp

Project Editor
Andy Beaster

Copy Editor
Damon Jordan

Indexer
Eric Schroeder

Proofreader
Tony Reitz

Team Coordinator
Amy Patton

Interior Designer
Gary Adair

Cover Designer
Jay Corpus

Copy Writer
Eric Borgert

Editorial Assistant
Angela Boley

Production
Brandon Allen
Susan Geiselman
Brad Lenser
Cheryl Lynch

Dedication

For my brother Pete, who claims to have taught me sports as a kid, but denounced the game of baseball when the strike cancelled a World Series. Now it's my turn—read this book and come back to the game, Pete.

Table of Contents

Acknowledgments

Thank you, thank you, a thousand times thank you, to Brenda Haugen, who compiled the two appendixes for me so that an early deadline could be met. I couldn't have done it without you.

I'd also like to thank Betsy Brown, my Acquisitions Editor on this book, for bringing me into the *Teach Yourself Today* series. As always, I'd like to thank Bev Eppink for acquiring me in the first place.

Some books have lengthy writing schedules, and some are tight. This one turned tight, and without a ton of help and, more importantly, understanding from my wife, Teri, I couldn't have completed it.

I'd like to take this opportunity to issue a couple of reminders to my children:

To Emily, my nine-year-old going on 16—remember that your Dad has the uncanny ability to cause embarrassment at the slightest provocation. It's my Super Power, and I'll use it if I have to.

To Robby and Sam, my twin six-year-olds—remember that for the time being, I'm still bigger than you. That means Tickle Torture for at least a few more years!

Rob Neyer would like to thank Eddie Epstein, Jay Mandel, John Marvel, and David Rawnsley for their help in making this book happen.

INTRODUCTION

Where We've Been, Where We Are, and Where We're Going (The Condensed Version)

Hi. I'm Rob Neyer, and I write a baseball column for ESPN.com, the most popular sports-related Web site on the Internet. People tend to assume that I'm an old hand at this Web stuff, but really, I'm not. Sure, I played around with America Online back in 1993, but it wasn't until 1996—when I was almost 30 years old—that I began using the Internet on a daily basis. And I'm sad to say that it was probably too late. That is, my habits had already become so ingrained that, four years later, I still sometimes forget to consult the Internet *first* when I need a piece of information.

Yet it's the Internet that has made my career, such as it is. I've now been writing the aforementioned daily column at ESPN.com for more than four years, and it just so happens that my writing style, conversational in the extreme, lends itself to the immediacy of the Internet. I can post a new column, receive a score of emails on that column, and post any corrections or clarifications that might be necessary—all within a few minutes. I read every email that comes in, and I also respond to many of them. The Internet has allowed me to establish relationships, however tenuous, with literally thousands of my readers, and I believe that makes all of us a bit happier than we might otherwise be.

An Infinite Variety of Experiences

A couple of years ago, I got to talking with a beautiful woman at a party, and she happened to ask me what I did for a living. When I told her I wrote about baseball, she immediately lost whatever slight interest she might have had in me. But for the sake of politeness, she asked, "I don't get it. What's so great about baseball?"

I began my reply with, "Baseball provides an infinite variety of experiences," quickly got bogged down and, as you might already have guessed, I never saw this particular beautiful woman again. Still, given enough time,

I think I could have convinced her. Because baseball really *does* provide an infinite variety of experiences.

You like numbers? Baseball's got 'em, coming out the kazoo and spilling all over the floor of your office. (Oops, that's the floor of *my* office!)

You like history? Jeez, baseball easily boasts the richest history of any American sport, and there's a minor cottage industry devoted to publishing books about the most obscure baseball-related topics imaginable.

You like daily drama? I've always maintained that, for eight months, baseball is sport's version of the soap opera, except that this one's even better because it runs on weekends.

You like athleticism? A lot of people watch figure skaters for the ballet-like quality of their performances, but I'll take Omar Vizquel and Roberto Alomar turning a double play any day. Or Ken Griffey perfectly timing his leap to steal a home run from an enemy batter, or Barry Bonds unleashing his fearsome swing and launching a 95-MPH fastball over the right-field fence.

You like movies? There have been more good movies involving baseball than all other sports combined.

You gave up trying to hit the curve ball years ago, but you still enjoy baseball-related competition? Well, a huge percentage of the game's individual events are recorded, thus the sport lends itself to all kinds of simulations and "shadow" games, from Strat-O-Matic (the former) to Rotisserie (the latter).

You like sitting in the sun and shooting the breeze with your best friend? What better place for this activity than the bleachers at Wrigley Field or Fenway Park on a perfect Sunday afternoon?

When it comes to enjoying baseball, I've just scratched the surface here. And of course, the wonderful thing about the Internet is that it allows us to enjoy baseball—however we might choose to enjoy our National Pastime—so much more easily. Alas, 'twas not always so....

The Dark Ages

If you were born after 1975, I suppose this will sound like ancient history, but there was a time when (*gasp!*) ESPN did not exist. I first began following baseball religiously in 1976. Allow me, for just a moment, to describe the lot of a baseball fan in those days.

At that time, I lived near Kansas City, so of course I listened to the Royals on the radio nearly every summer evening. (Occasionally, a road game would be broadcast on TV, but that was a special treat.) If I wanted to actually see any of the night's action, I would have to wait until about 10:20, when a local sportscaster might favor us with a few timely hits. He'd give us the scores from the other games, too, but only in passing. For any details of those other games, we had two choices: We could continue listening to the radio, where eventually Fred White would give the scores of the other games, along with the names of the winning and losing pitchers; and/or we could wait until the next morning for the sports section in the local newspaper (an eternity for an obsessive).

This was, it must be said, little different from the experiences of baseball fans 20 years earlier. In fact, between the widespread introduction of television in the early 1950s and the explosion of cable television in the late 1970s, virtually nothing changed for baseball fans. You listened to the game on the radio or perhaps watched the broadcast on TV, and in the morning you woke up with the box scores (and unless you lived on the West Coast, you weren't privy to the results of many of the previous night's games because they hadn't been completed before your newspaper went to press).

It was all we had, so we liked it. Hell, we loved it. Baseball's such a wonderful game, it's great even if you're reading about it the next day. But then came cable television, and suddenly it became a little easier to develop an obsession with the sport. In addition to ESPN's SportsCenter, which gave us the highlights that had been so sorely missing for so long from the local news, cable also brought us the so-called "superstations." In my little corner of the world, the superstations brought us the Braves and Cubs, hundreds of times per season. Finally, those of us who lived in American League cities got to see, on a regular basis, National League stars such as Mike Schmidt and Pete Rose and Steve Garvey and Dave Parker and Gary Carter and Steve Carlton. Sure, this might have taken away a little luster from the All-Star Game, but what a great tradeoff!

Things didn't change much in the 1980s, but toward the end of the decade, ESPN started broadcasting baseball games—for a few years, they broadcast a *lot* of baseball games—along with *Baseball Tonight* (my all-time favorite TV program). And Life Was Good. But of course, you still had to wait until the next morning for the box scores, and if you owned a

Rotisserie baseball team, as so many of us did (and do), the wait drove you nuts.

And then *it* happened. There's no neat little date to which we can refer and say, "That's when the Internet got big." But I think it's safe to say that many people first experienced the new world online in the early 1990s, in one form or another. Fortunately for the publishers of this book, that process continues today, and shows few signs of letting up.

The New Era

And now, here we are. It's funny, quite often we think of the Internet as a time-saving device, and it certainly is that. If your favorite band has just released a new CD, it's quite a bit quicker to order it from CDNOW (*www.cdnow.com*) than to schlep down to your local record store, where they might not even have the disc you want. If you need to compare three models of cars, doing the research online is a lot faster than driving around town to all the dealerships.

But for rabid baseball fans, I suspect, access to the Internet doesn't mean less time following the game, it probably means *more* time—and certainly more information. For me, that's really the beauty of the Internet. Whereas 10 years ago, I might have read the standings and the box scores the next morning in my local paper and caught a few highlights on SportsCenter, now I can see all those things on the Internet when I *want* to see them. And the future? Anybody who guesses correctly is just lucky, but it probably won't be long before we have access to any part of any major league game, any time we like. And after that happens, something even better will come along. I feel incredibly lucky that I'll be here to see it, whatever "it" may be.

Postscript

Before I let you go, just a few words of advice. This book will likely serve as your introduction to the incredible amount of baseball content that's available on the Internet, and I think it will serve you quite well. But if you're stuck, or you somehow think of something baseball-related that is *not* in this book, then your first destination should be John Skilton's Baseball Links (*www.baseball-links.com*). It's the site of last—and quite often, first—resort for nearly all experienced Web-surfers-slash-baseball fans. Armed with this knowledge, I bid you go forth. And I envy you, just a little, for the thrill of discovery that's to come.

PART I

Stepping Up to the Plate

CHAPTER 1

Learning the Rules Online

What better place to start than with the rules of the game?

Those of you who have played, watched, and loved the game of baseball for years may look at this chapter title and say, "Aw, heck, I can skip that one. I *know* the rules." You may very well know the rules, but you should still find this chapter to be of value. (Pssssst. If you are relatively new to the game, this chapter *will* show you where to find the rules.)

We're going to assume—despite the dangerous consequences that often brings—that you know the basic rules of the game of baseball. So I'm not going to force you to read through pages upon pages of balls, strikes, outs, runs, hits, and errors.

But baseball, perhaps more than any of the other major sports, has tons of obscure rules. If you want to start an argument, all you have to do is walk into a sports bar and ask three people to explain the infield fly rule to you.

Plus, baseball rules differ (wildly, in some cases) between levels. Professionals play with one set of rules, colleges use another, and American Legion and Little League each has its own set of rules as well. The basics are the same, but many rules and interpretations of rules vary.

So, if you have a question about a rule, what are you going to do?

That's what this chapter is all about. We'll start with a tour of the Major League Baseball rules—the ones that apply when you're watching the Yankees win yet another World Series. The big leaguers all play by the same rules (except for the designated hitter, of course), and they're all listed on the Web.

What You'll Learn in This Chapter:

- ▶ How to find and use the Major League Baseball rulebook on the Web.
- ▶ How to find the American Legion rulebook.
- ▶ Where you can find rules for Little League organizations.
- ▶ How to find an umpire association.

Here's the Scoop:
Catcher's interference is when the catcher inhibits a batter's swing in some way. For example, if the catcher sticks his glove out too far and the batter hits it with the bat. The batter is awarded first base, and the catcher has a really sore hand.

Next, we'll jump down a few levels and locate the rules for some teenage players who play American Legion baseball around the country.

We'll also take a look at the Little League rules that are in use during the annual Little League World Series in Williamsport, Pennsylvania, and find out where you can find rules for local organizations.

Finally, for you umpires (or umpire-wannabes) out there, we'll take a look at an umpires' association on the Internet.

Major League Baseball Rules

What happens when a batted ball strikes an umpire? How long must a player hold the ball in his glove for it to be considered a legal catch? What the heck is catcher's interference?

These are all good questions. A less-interested party might answer them with a quick, "Who cares?" Spend any time around the game, however, and you'll come in contact with these plays. It's helpful to know what the rule is when you do.

> **Go to the source:**
> If you do any research on the Web for baseball rules, you'll probably come across a number of sites that claim to offer the "official" rules of Major League Baseball. This is true for a variety of different subjects on the Web.
>
> Just because a site claims to be "official" doesn't make it so. Many of these sites might indeed provide reliable information, but when I'm online, I like to go to the source of the information whenever possible.
>
> So, when we look for the Major League Baseball rules, we're going to start with the Major League Baseball site.

The official major league rules govern the American and National Leagues as well as any other league that is a member of the National Association of Professional Baseball Leagues. Most of these "other" leagues are the minor leagues that are affiliated with Major League Baseball.

Many leagues that are unaffiliated with the major leagues also use these rules, so you might see them in play elsewhere. Also, many youth leagues or adult amateur leagues will have in their rules that they "follow the rules of Major League Baseball, with a few exceptions." This way, they don't have to print their own rulebook. They just make note of what rules are different from those used by the big leaguers.

So let's start by going to the major leagues' official Web site at *www.majorleaguebaseball.com* and check out the rules.

Neyer's Nuggets

Neyer's Nugget: Knotty Problems:

For the most part, baseball fans assume that they know all the rules—or that at least they know all the rules they need to know. Watch enough baseball, however, and eventually you'll run into all sorts of what *The Sporting News* used to call "Baseball's Knotty Problems." When I first began writing my ESPN.com column in 1996, questions about rules were frequent. In response to queries from readers, I wrote about batted balls, kicked balls, lost balls[el]you name it. In fact, it reached the point where many readers treated my column as something as a public utility, emailing me their questions before making any real efforts to find the answers on their own (you'd be surprised how many long-term baseball fans really *don't* know the infield-fly rule). And the balk rule? I've been obsessed with baseball since I was ten years old, and that one is still a mystery to me.

Before long, I began doing what the author of this book has done: I referred all these curious readers to *www.majorleaguebaseball.com*, where the entire *Official Rules of Baseball* can be so easily accessed. As an added bonus, beginning in the 2000 season, majorleaguebaseball.com will feature a regular question-and-answer section on the rules of the game, with users supplying the questions, and actual major-league umpires supplying the answers. Welcome back, Knotty Problems!

Using the Official Major League Rule Book

Once you've gotten to the Major League Baseball home page, finding the rules is easy. Down the left side of the home page, you'll see a button called "Official Info." Click on it, and you'll open a page that highlights the address of the Office of the Commissioner of Baseball. Scroll down the page until you see a link called, "Official Rules." Click it, and you'll see a page that looks like the following figure.

*Clicking on
Official Info but-
ton will bring you
to this page.*

This is an index of the actual rules that are used in real major-
league games, all summer long. So, if you're at a game or
watching one on television and something happens that you
don't understand, you can come here to find your answer.

Or, if you are a relative newcomer to baseball, you can read the
entire rule book if you wish!

> **Layout of the Rules:**
>
> Major-league rules are laid out in a numerical "code" that is divided
> into 10 major categories, including "Objectives of the Game, the Playing
> Field, Equipment," and "The Official Scorer," to name a few.
>
> Each rule has an official number. It's a little like the Dewey Decimal
> System. For example, all the rules that cover pitching are in the 8.00
> group, such as Rule 8.05, which describes when a balk should be called.

Searching through the Major-League Rules

Let's take a look through the major-league rules and try to find
the answer to that pesky bar-brawl question I posed in the
introduction to this chapter: What is the infield fly rule?

One problem with the official major-league site is that it doesn't
offer you the ability to search through the rules to find a particular topic. So, you're forced to work your way through the index
to find your topic.

You may have already known that the infield fly rule pertains to a batted ball, so you might try to find its explanation under 6.00, The Batter. You'd be wrong.

1. Go to the main major-league site at *www.majorleaguebaseball.com*, as you had done before. Click on the Official Info button on the left side of the screen.

2. Scroll down the Official Info page until you see the Official Rules link. Click it.

3. On the main Major League Baseball Rules page, click Definition of Terms. It is category 2.00 in the official code.

4. The terms are listed in alphabetical order. Scroll down until you find Infield Fly Rule. There's your explanation.

▼ **Try It Yourself**

▲

The Definition of Terms section of the rules is invaluable for explaining a lot about the game. The other rules will explain how these terms are applied in a game, but the explanation of such things as a balk, a fielder's choice, obstruction, and so on, are found in the Definition of Terms.

The Infield Fly Rule:
The infield fly rule exists to protect baserunners in the event of a pop fly in the infield. Since a baserunner must stay close to his base on a pop-up with less than two outs, an infielder might be tempted to let the pop-up drop and attempt to get more than one force-out.

So, if first and second bases are occupied, there are less than two outs, and a pop-up occurs in the infield, an umpire should call out "infield fly." At that point, the batter is automatically out, regardless of whether the ball is caught. Runners can still advance after a catch, but don't have to.

The Rules of American Legion Baseball

American Legion baseball was first played in 1925. High-school age players from across the nation play American Legion baseball, typically during the summer after their high school teams' seasons have ended.

According to the American Legion, nearly 95,000 players participated in the program in 1999. Players are age 15-18, and a local American Legion Post sponsors their teams.

By the Way:

American Legion baseball is a program of the American Legion, the national association for veterans of military service. As such, the American Legion baseball Web site is actually part of a larger site for the American Legion itself.

There are other programs for this and other age levels to play—Amateur Athletic Union (AAU), Babe Ruth, Connie Mack, Mickey Mantle, Little League (covered later in this chapter), and PONY Baseball, just to name a few. Each has its own set of official rules.

Let's use American Legion as an example, since it is the largest baseball program for high-school aged kids.

The American Legion baseball site itself is not very pretty to look at, but it's chock full of information. You can see it by going to the following Web address: *www.legion.org/BASEBALL/ home.htm*. It is shown in the following figure.

The American Legion Baseball site has a link for rules.

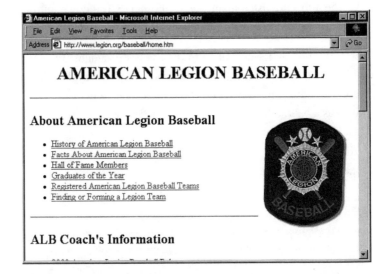

Unlike the major-league rules, the American Legion rules can't just be read online. Instead, they are in a PDF format that requires you to download the rules file and then view it on your computer. The good news is that once you've done that, you can view the rules any time you want, whether you are online or not.

Download Acrobat

In order to view the PDF rules file, you'll need Adobe Acrobat Reader installed on your computer. Acrobat Reader is a free program, and the American Legion provides you with a button that links you to the Adobe site, where you will find instructions for downloading and installing Acrobat Reader.

1. Start at the American Legion baseball site at *www.legion.org/BASEBALL/home.htm.*

2. Click on the rules link, found under ALB Coach's Information.

3. To download the file, click on the link to the rules on the rules page. Once the file is downloaded (and assuming you have Acrobat Reader installed), you can open it on your computer any time you want.

▼ **Try It Yourself**

▲

Little League Rules

Little League baseball is everywhere. It's played all over the country by thousands of children. In many cases, it's simple fun. In some areas, it's serious stuff.

Little League Baseball is actually a national organization that crowns a national champion in several age divisions. Little League holds a World Series that, unlike Major League Baseball, is a true *world* series, giving children from around the globe a chance to play for the title.

The annual World Series for those age 12 and under is held in Williamsport, Pennsylvania, and is televised nationally. Little League Baseball maintains official rules that apply to the World Series. Most local Little League organizations follow these rules.

Little League Baseball also maintains an official web page at *www.littleleague.org.* However, you can't view or download the official Little League rules there (as of this writing, at least). These rules are much like the American Legion rules we found earlier in this chapter.

Many times, rules away from the games themselves are just as important when it comes to Little League organizations. By "away from the game," I mean rules about coaching, player eligibility, parent involvement, and so on, which often impact the success or failure of a youth league organization.

If your local organization maintains a web site, check it out for rules that may apply to your child's team. Often, you'll find a code of conduct for parents.

Let's take a look at one such site. The Union Park Little League organization of Orlando, Florida maintains a Web site at *www.upll.org*, as you can see in the following figure.

The Union Park Little League organization maintains a Web site that includes league rules.

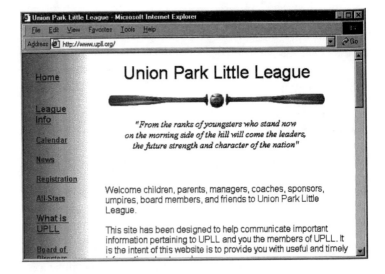

To get to the page that includes information on parent involvement, you just click the Getting Involved link on the left side of the page.

You can chose a division, click on its name, and you'll get a list of rules. These will include some playing rules, but much of these rules are code-of-conduct and other items that don't cover the game itself.

When it comes to youth sports, however, these rules can be just as important as any infield fly rule might be.

One Man's Opinion:

If your local youth baseball association doesn't have a code of conduct for parents or rules that apply to behavior of parents and players, you should lobby for one. Search the web for Little League organizations and use their rules to help you build some of your own. There's nothing worse than out-of-control youth sports parents.

Finding an Umpiring Association

"Kill the Ump!" might be the battle cry of the angry fan, but without good umpires, baseball would suffer. Whether you are already an umpire or want to be one someday, there are resources for you on the Web.

If your local umpiring association maintains a web site, that is often a good place to visit to get information. There are also several other regional and national sites that can be of value to umpires.

The Amateur Baseball Umpires Association keeps a Web site at *www.abua.com* (shown in the following figure). It's a relatively new organization, but it is dedicated to improving the quality of officiating throughout the country.

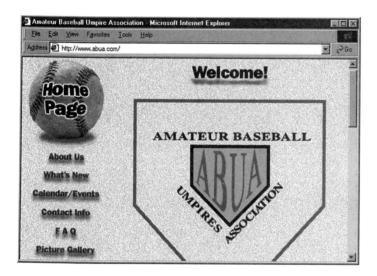

The Amateur Baseball Umpires Association's web site is a service for umps at all levels.

At *www.umpire.org*, an offshoot of the ABUA site, you'll find lots of resources for umpires, including links to umpire sites at the NCAA and major-league levels.

And speaking of the major-league umpires, you can visit their association's web site at *www.majorleagueumps.com*.

Rounding the Bases

You've made it all the way through one chapter. We're off to a pretty good start, if I do say so myself! In this chapter, we covered:

- The Major League Baseball rule book—where to find it and how to use it.

- American Legion Baseball's rules and how to download them from the Web.

- How to track down a local Little League organization's Web site and locate rules that are specific to it.

- How to find information for and about umpires at a variety of different levels of play.

CHAPTER 2

Coaching and Equipment

Now that you've spent an entire chapter (and, I hope, some time on your own) learning about the rules of the game, you're probably ready to be a coach, right? Or at least you *think* you're ready to be a coach.

As someone who has coached baseball at a variety of levels, I can tell you that no matter how prepared you think you are, there's always a little more work you could do. That's why there are so many successful coaching clinics around the country—coaches like to learn from each other.

You can do that on the Internet, too. There are many resources on the Web for coaching technique, drills, instruction, and so on. You can find everything from the right way to teach a youngster to throw a curveball to the right way to execute the hit-and-run.

We'll start by looking at a couple of sites from which you can get advice from people with major-league experience. Then, we'll look at a great place for the coach of youth-level teams to get some sound coaching advice. We'll even look at a more professorial approach to coaching advice.

Next, we'll take a look at support services for coaches— coaching associations. We'll walk through some examples of association Web sites and see what they can offer.

Then it's time to find some baseball equipment on the Internet. We'll look at some gadgets that coaches can use to help players develop. We'll see some places where you can find the basic equipment for the game, too—bats, balls, gloves, spikes, and even the bases themselves.

What You'll Learn in This Chapter:

▶ Where to look for advice from major-league coaches or players with major-league experience.

▶ Where to find some coaching resources for amateur coaches at all levels.

▶ How coaches associations use the Internet for the members.

▶ Where to find some unique training devices for player development.

▶ Some places in which you can find the basic equipment that every baseball team needs.

Watch for Commercial Interruptions:

Many of the sites that we'll look at in this chapter have some sort of commercial hook to them. A coach, for example, may offer a few hints or tips for coaches on the site to entice them to buy their book or series of videotapes. There's nothing wrong with that, of course, but remember to exercise caution as you surf.

Help for Coaches

Some coaches are less willing to admit it than others, but all coaches can use help from their peers and the pros from time to time. Whether it's an idea to help with in-game strategy or a new drill that might help your infielders a little, every little bit helps.

The Web is a great resource for ideas for coaches. You can find help for coaching players at every level, from teaching the little ones which base is which to teaching the proper cutoff positioning for your American Legion team's defense.

Some sites are better than others at providing the information you need. Some will offer a ton of information right at your fingertips, while others will simply try to lure you into buying their videotapes. It's up to you to find the value, regardless of which type of site you visit.

Getting Some Help from the Pros

It can't hurt to get some advice from people who've played or coached the game at its highest level. That's what this section is all about.

Any decent search of the Web will yield plenty of sites from professional players and managers who want a piece of your pocketbook. Some of those are very valuable sites indeed. But the best ones on the Web are those that are regularly updated with new information and offer something for the coach or player who just happens to drop by.

Dick Mills' pitching site (*www.pitching.com*) is a good example of the latter. Mills, a former pitcher for the Boston Red Sox, believes that pitchers are made in the off-season. He calls the four key areas of pitching, "developing a compact yet powerful delivery, building a strong arm, pitching-specific strength and conditioning, and mental toughness training." Check it out in the following figure.

Mills has put his technique into practice in his own home. His son, Ryan, pitched at Arizona State and was drafted by the Minnesota Twins with the sixth overall pick in the 1998 amateur draft.

Dick Mills' All About Pitching offers advice for young hurlers, their coaches, and parents.

Mills offers a free pitching report (ordered by email) and other items of interest for pitchers and pitching coaches.

For example, click on the Throwing/Bullpen link, and you'll get some great advice for pitchers, including a sample weekly throwing schedule that will help prevent arm injuries to your young players.

Neyer's Nuggets

Neyer's Nugget: Ryan Mills, Where Are You?

Whatever happened to Ryan Mills? Well, Dick Mills's son is still only 22 years old, but so far the news has not been good. In 1998, the Minnesota Twins selected Ryan with the sixth pick in the first round of the amateur draft, on the strength of his 95-MPH fastball and knee-buckling curve. He signed a contract, reported to Minnesota's farm team in Florida—and promptly came down with a sore arm, the result of horrific over-work when he was pitching for Arizona State.

Mills returned to the mound in 1999 and went 3-10 with—are you ready for this?—an 8.87 earned-run average. He had great stuff, throwing 95 MPH every game, but perhaps because he was thousands of miles away from his father, Ryan lost confidence in his mechanics and couldn't get them right.

continues

continued

What, if anything, does this mean? First, perhaps we should take what Dick Mills says about pitching mechanics and preventing arm injuries with a grain of salt. Second, and more important, is a great lesson for all of us: Pitchers are incredibly fragile, and teams that spend high draft picks on such pitchers often wind up regretting it, especially when those pitchers were abused in college.

You may have never heard of Wendell Kim, but he's the third-base coach for the Boston Red Sox. He's got his own Web site that, if nothing else, offers some insight into what a major-league coach experiences.

Kim's site (*www.wk20.com*) includes a diary of his experiences throughout a season and a complete account of what a coaching staff does in preparation for a game, among other things.

Perhaps the best part of this site is the "You Be the Coach" area. Here, Kim offers a scenario that occurred during an actual game and asks you to explain how you would handle it and why. Since he's the third base coach, many of these situations are of the baserunning variety, but it's interesting and fun.

There's even a complete archive of previous "You Be the Coach" segments. These are fun because you can read some responses from other users of the site as well as Kim's response to the situation.

Amateurs Helping Amateurs

Anyone who's ever coached for any length of time probably has come up with an idea that might be helpful to other coaches. It might be a special drill, or a way of handling troublesome parents, or a strategic move.

Regardless, we can all help each other. And, we can do it on the Internet.

One top-notch Internet site for amateur coaches is at *eteamz.com*, a site devoted solely to supporting those who play the games for fun.

The baseball instruction area of Eteamz is located at *www.eteamz.com/baseball/instruction/*. You can see it in the following figure.

There's a special area for coaching tee ball and clinics online for pitching, catching and more. You can even enter a chat area and talk with other coaches in real time, using a "whiteboard" to draw out examples of what you're talking about.

One Man's Opinion:
Eteamz is set up for much more than just baseball, and any amateur athlete, coach or administrator could benefit from spending a couple of hours perusing the site.

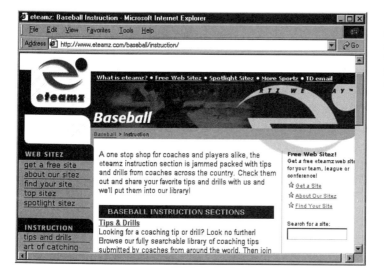

The baseball instruction area of Eteamz is packed with tips for coaches and players.

The most useful area of this site might just be the archive of tips and drills that have been submitted by coaches from across the country. It's fully searchable, so if you're looking for something to help with baserunning, you can find help quickly. You can also submit your own drills and ideas for other coaches to look over.

It's a great resource for coaches; just make sure your cross-town rivals don't hear about it!

Let's take a look at how you'd find drills on turning a double play.

1. From the Eteamz baseball instruction page at the address given above, click on the Tips & Drills link.

2. You'll get a list of baseball categories, you can select one of them that fits your topic of interest, or you can enter your topic in the search field below. For the sake of this example, click on Fielding.

3. A long list of drills appears in alphabetical order. Scroll down, and you'll see a drill called Double Play Drill. Click that link.

4. A screen opens that explains how to run a double-play drill. You're ready to go!

▲

A great resource for a different kind of advice for coaches are the many universities around the country that publish articles on the Web on topics ranging from the mechanics of the curveball to sports injuries and so on.

You'll find one such example from Virginia Tech University at *www.chre.vt.edu/f-s/rstratto/CYS/*. It's a newsletter published as a public service to help coaches of all sports be better prepared to do their jobs. There's a lot of this type of material out there on the Web, it's just a matter of finding it. I found this site particularly interesting.

Finding Associations for Coaches

By the Way:

A great place to start in looking for an association is by searching the Internet. However, in many cases you'll find what you're looking for more quickly using another source, like a printed directory or regional magazine that might print the addresses of area associations for coaches.

There are associations for coaches all over the country, at all different levels. Some of them are just for baseball coaches, while others are for coaches of all different sports at a particular level, such as a high school coaches association.

Even if they aren't just for baseball coaches, there's a lot to gain from joining a coaches association. Many times, you can benefit from an association's Web site regardless of whether you are a member.

Finding coaches associations can be tricky, because Internet search engines often miss them. When you find them, though, there's a lot to gain.

Let's take a look at a couple of them. The best place to start is the National High School Athletic Coaches Association site at *www.hscoaches.org*. You can get a glimpse of it in the following figure.

Here you'll find a lot of information about the organization itself, and about upcoming events for coaches of all sports. On the home page is a link to a nomination form for the U.S. Navy's Scholastic All-America team for several sports, including baseball. You can also learn about upcoming conferences and coaches' meetings.

You'll also find codes of conduct for coaches and parents on the site.

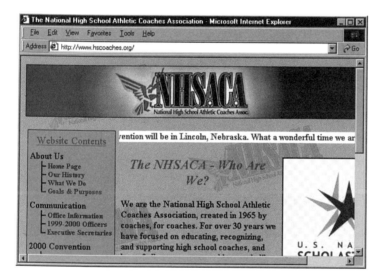

The National High School Athletic Coaches Association's Web site.

A good example of a more local coaches association is the Illinois Coaches Association (*http://members.accessus.net/~icacoach/*). The site exists to support coaches of all sports, and lists the names of the chairmen of each of individual sport in the state.

You can also find forms where coaches can nominate their players for statewide all-star competitions in a variety of sports, including baseball.

If you look carefully enough, you can find associations for Little League coaches, American Legion coaches, and so on. Some of them require memberships in order for you to access certain areas of their sites, while others don't require any membership fee at all. Happy hunting!

Equipping Your Team

One Man's Opinion:

For information on a very necessary part of any baseball player's existence—sunflower seeds—check out the Fisher Web site at *www.jbssinc.com.*

If you're going to coach a baseball team at any level you're going to need a few things. First, there are the essentials—bats, balls, gloves, uniforms, helmets, and so on. Then, there are the extras, such as fungo bats, pine-tar rags, bat weights, maybe even a pitching machine. If you're really going to go after it, you might even want to try a gimmick or two, such as swing trainers, facemasks, or a special helmet that keeps a hitter's eye on the ball.

There's plenty of equipment—necessary and not—for baseball teams. On the Internet, there's a seemingly endless supply of places to find it.

Check the Major Retailers:

The sites listed here are just the tip of the iceberg when it comes to buying baseball equipment online. You might want to try a somewhat more traditional source for equipment—a major retailer.

Any major sporting goods store worth its weight in pine tar has a Web site. You can search for them by name, but one safe bet would be to take the retailer's name and sticking it between *www.* and *.com*. You're pretty likely to find what you're looking for.

Getting Equipment from an e-Tailer

Let's take a look at a couple of Web sites that aren't associated with traditional retailers. Since the Internet explosion began in the mid-90s, more and more such companies have sprung up on the Web.

Baseball Depot is one of them (*www.baseballdepot.com*). Through this site, you can find just about anything you need in the baseball world. However, the list of manufacturers whose products are available is somewhat limited.

Let's take a trip through this site and quickly try to find some baseball pants .

Try It Yourself ▼

1. When you type in the Baseball Depot address, you are taken to a sort of cover page for the site.

2. Click the Baseball Depot link to enter the site. You will see a page like the one you see in the following figure.

3. Click on the Apparel button, and you'll get a list of products—many of them baseball pants—which you can purchase.

Another good example of a baseball e-tailer is 123 Baseball (*www.123-baseball.com*). It's another great place to find the equipment for which you're looking. Take some time to browse around this site—you'll like what you see.

The Baseball Depot site offers equipment and apparel for sale.

Try a Gimmick or Two

Do any search for baseball equipment on the Internet and a large share of the results will be sites that hawk the latest and greatest in baseball gimmicks.

It might be a trainer that allows your players to feel comfortable keeping their heads down on a grounder. It might be a swing trainer. There are tons of them. It's up to you to determine which ones might be for you (if any).

The Zip Baseball Trainer (*www.ziptrainer.com*) is one of many such sites. It claims to improve the throwing mechanics of all players, including pitchers learning to throw a curveball.

Another such site advertises the Accubat (*www.americanmold.com/accubat/*). It's roughly a cross between a fungo bat and a racquet-ball racquet, allowing coaches to hit consistent grounders and pop-ups to players so they don't spend so much time chasing down miss-hits.

These are just a pair of examples out of dozens of such sites. Take a look around the Web when you get time, and you'll find many more.

Rounding the Bases

Now you're ready to coach a team of your own! In this chapter, we covered:

- Finding coaching advice from professionals.

- Using the Internet to get information on drills and other coaching advice for youth coaches.

- How to look for coaching associations on the Internet and what they typically offer.

- How to shop for equipment for your team—everything from balls to specialty products.

CHAPTER 3

Development of the Game

There's an old saying that goes something like: We can't know where we're going unless we understand where we've been.

Now, we can sit and argue the merits of that statement until we're blue in the face, but it's an old saying, so it's worth considering, at least.

Baseball has a longer history than any of the major professional sports in America. The major leagues date back well before the turn of the century (the *previous* turn of the century, that is).

Of course, the game we see on the field today is markedly different from the game that was played years ago. But perhaps more than any other sport, baseball's fans tend to latch on to history. That might be because the history of the game is so deep and rich.

In fact, many of the most important societal changes in the 20th Century were mirrored in the game of baseball. Everything from integration to high tech manufacturing processses has had major impacts on both society and the game of baseball.

But let's not get too preachy here. This chapter should be fun, and I think you'll find that it will be.

This chapter will focus on baseball's history. We'll start with the major leagues, but we'll go well beyond them as well. We'll take a look at a couple of different ways to pursue major-league history online.

In addition to straight major-league history, we'll also take a gander at World Series history sites and how to find specific historical information about players and teams from the past.

What You'll Learn in This Chapter:

▶ Some great places to find information about the history of the major leagues—everything from standings to statistics to stories.

▶ Where you can find information about the World Series from years gone by.

▶ Some ideas on how you can learn more about your favorite players and teams from the past.

▶ How to find out more about the Negro Leagues from the pre-integration era of baseball.

▶ Where you can find more information about the All-American Girls Professional Baseball League.

Then, we'll go away from the major leagues to look at baseball's "other" league from before Jackie Robinson broke the color barrier—the Negro Leagues. There are some great historical sites about the Negro Leagues, and it's a subject that is understudied and under-appreciated by much of this generation of fans.

Finally, we'll look at the short-lived All-American Girls Professional Baseball League, the one popularized by the recent movie, *A League of Their Own.*

Major League Baseball History

Depending on your age and, perhaps, where you live, the "glory days" of baseball can be at any point on the calendar. It might have been the 20s (Babe Ruth and the Yankees) the 50s (Mickey Mantle and the Yankees), the 70s (Reggie Jackson and the A's and Yankees), or the 90s (again, the Yankees).

There are people, of course, who aren't Yankee fans. For those of us in the Twin Cities, the glory days of baseball were from 1987-91, when the Twins won two World Series.

But whether your idea of a slugger is Mark McGwire, Hank Aaron, or Babe Ruth (or all three), you can find a lot of history on the Internet.

Major-league History as Provided by Major League Baseball

It seems only natural to begin a search for historical facts about the game of baseball with a visit to the official site of the major leagues at *www.majorleaguebaseball.com.*

All you have to do it click on the history button on the left side of the screen, and you'll be taken to the history section of the site, as shown in the following figure.

This area is full of stats, player bios and other historical information. As the figure indicates, the page is actually called, "History and Records." This site would be a great place to build a list of historical facts for a research paper, because there is a lot of factual information to be found.

Major League Baseball offers detailed historical facts.

Neyer's Nugget: Holtzman Saves

When you want history, sometimes there's nothing better than an eyewitness account. And when it comes to eyewitness accounts, there are few writers alive who have seen more baseball than Jerome Holtzman, who was hired by Major League Baseball in 1999, to fill the brand-new position of "Official Baseball Historian." In part, Holtzman's job is to help MLB decide on statistical issues from baseball's (sometimes) murky past. As an example, he submitted a report to the Commissioner's Office on the events related to the lifetime suspension of Shoeless Joe Jackson.

Fortunately for devotees of the game's incredibly rich history, Holtzman's duties also include a regular column at MLB's Web site (*www.majorleaguebaseball.com*) where, in 1999, he wrote on a variety of subjects including the revision of Hack Wilson's 1930 RBI record, the legacy of Twins owner Calvin Griffith, and—a subject dear to my heart—bases-loaded intentional walks. Holtzman also wrote about the invention of the "save" statistic.

Holtzman was uniquely positioned to write about saves; he's the man who invented the statistic. If you include his early work as a sports-department copyboy, Holtzman's been covering baseball for nearly six decades, almost all of that with first the *Chicago Sun-Times* and later the *Chicago Tribune*. In that time span, Holtzman estimates, "I've seen

continues

continued

> somewhere in the neighborhood of seven thousand major
> league games, including spring training and postseason."
> During the 2000 season, the indefatigable columnist will be
> writing columns, mostly history oriented, approximately
> every two weeks. So why are young Web surfers of the 21st
> century so interested in what happened way back in the
> 20th century? Holtzman answers simply, "Baseball has the
> best history."
>
> And now, MLB's Web site has one of baseball's best writers.

The concentration is on records—and lots of them. You can see the career leaders in every statistical category you can think of, and see all the game's records.

Franchise Histories:

Later in this chapter, we'll look at some places where you *can* learn more about the histories of various franchises.

The site does offer depth in some areas, but doesn't go deep enough in others. For example, there's a whole section on baseball commissioners, in which you can read biographies of everyone from Kenesaw Mountain Landis to Bud Selig. You can even read a detailed history of the commissionership itself.

But when you visit the Franchise Histories page, you would probably love to be able to read detailed histories of every franchise. Instead, you get a list of franchises and the dates they were (or are) in existence, with no other information available.

One of the best parts of this site is the Miscellaneous category. You can learn about father-son combinations, view historical video, and more.

Let's have some fun and take a listen to Dick Stockton's call of Carlton Fisk's homer in Game 6 of the 1975 World Series .

Try It Yourself ▼

1. Go to the Major League Baseball Web site at *www. majorleaguebaseball.com*. In the index on the left side of the page, click History.

2. Scroll down the History and Records page to the Miscellaneous category and click on the link to Historic Broadcast Calls.

3. Scroll down the page to the year 1975, and click on either the Real Audio or Windows Media link to the sound clip. It will download and play automatically.

Getting the Total Story at Total Baseball

Another detailed historical baseball site can be found at Total Baseball Online (*www.totalbaseball.com*). When you get to the main home page, just click the History button at the top of the screen and you'll move to the history page, as seen in the following figure.

Want to go beyond the stats and scores and learn more about the intricate detail that went into the formation of the record book? This is the site for you.

Here, you'll not only find the stats that both settle and create baseball arguments, you can learn how the stats got created in the first place.

Download the Audio Program:

If you don't have either Real Audio or Windows Media Player, you can download one or both from this page. At the top of the Historic Broadcast Calls page are buttons that link you to sites where those programs can be downloaded.

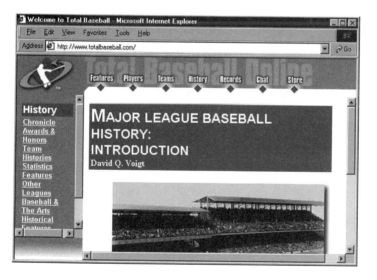

Total Baseball offers another perspective on major-league history.

Total Baseball Online opens with a brief introduction in the main page. On the left side is a menu with links to other historical pages within Total Baseball.

If you want to learn about statistics, just click the Statistics Features link. There, you can read about Henry Chadwick, the first person to chart more about a baseball game than wins and losses, outs, and runs.

This is the best site I've come across for providing an encyclopedia-style look at the history of the game. Let's take a quick walk through that history by reading about the many ways the game has changed from its origins to today.

Try It Yourself ▼

1. From the Total Baseball Online site (*www.totalbaseball.com*), click the History button at the top of the page.

2. In the menu at the left side of the screen, click the Historical Features link.

3. A new menu appears at the left. Click The Changing Game.

4. In the menu that appears next, you can take your pick of the topic you wish to learn more about, everything from equipment to night baseball to strategy.

▲

One Man's Opinion:

He may not be the greatest player ever to play the game—then again, he may be—but I've got Roberto Clemente at the top of my list of favorite players. His 3,000 hits and numerous gold gloves only scratched the surface of the kind of player he was. His death in a plane crash while flying relief supplies to earthquake-ravaged Nicaragua in 1972 goes a long way toward explaining the kind of man he was.

The Histories of Individual Franchises

Which franchise has been in one city longer than any other? Whether you knew the answer or not (it's the Chicago Cubs) you could have learned that and more at Total Baseball Online.

On the main history page, you can click on a link to Team Histories in the menu at the left of the screen. That menu then changes and includes the names of every franchise that is currently in the major leagues.

The individual histories are very thorough, complete with the highs and lows of each team's existence. These histories aren't terribly up-to-date (through 1996 as of this writing), but this isn't really about *recent* history, anyway.

It's even fun to look back on the histories of the younger franchises. For example, the San Diego Padres history takes you from its beginnings in 1969 through history and the likes of Nate Colbert, Dave Winfield, Randy Jones, and Tony Gwynn.

It's great reading.

Using the Baseball Almanac

Another site you might like to swing though is the Baseball Almanac at *www.baseball-almanac.com*.

There's a lot here other than history, but you can check out some of the historical information as well. Don't come here looking for the straight history of the game or the major leagues, but for the more off-beat stuff.

For example, there's a Famous Firsts page that leads to a list of the first player or team to accomplish this or that. There's even a U.S. Presidents page that explains the connection to the game that many presidents felt, and contains links to famous quotations from them.

It's a fun place to visit.

Learning about the Negro Leagues

Imagine, if you can, the major leagues today without such stars as Ken Griffey, Jr. What if the major leagues had never seen Hank Aaron, Bob Gibson, or Kirby Puckett? Would the games have been as good?

That one's easy to answer. It's amazing to think that African American players had to form their own leagues at one point in our country's history. What might be more amazing is to think how the major leagues might have been had the great stars of the Negro Leagues been allowed to play with and against their white counterparts.

It took a long time for Negro League accomplishments to be mentioned alongside those of major league players. Today, however, there are 16 Negro League players in the Hall of Fame in Cooperstown, N.Y. Major League Baseball's Web site has a Negro League section in it. Still, much of the Negro League's history is unknown by the average baseball fan.

If you're curious about what the Negro Leagues were all about, a good place to start your study of the topic is Negro League Baseball Dot Com, which is located, of course, at *www.negroleaguebaseball.com.* You can see the home page in the following figure.

The Negro Leagues—and there were several different leagues that fall under that category—existed early in the 1900s, dying out in the 40s when the top stars began to make their way onto major-league rosters.

Negro League Baseball Dot Com offers a wealth of background information on the leagues.

One Man's Opinion:

You can't call yourself a fan of baseball history if you have excluded the Negro Leagues from your study. If you haven't spent much time reading about them, you'll probably be amazed at what you'll find. My guess is you'll come away with a new appreciation for the players of that era.

Many great players, from Satchel Paige to Josh Gibson, highlighted the highest level of the Negro Leagues. This site details their exploits, and keeps it fun for fans as well with a variety of different contests and quizzes.

A good place to start is the FAQ section, especially if you don't have a lot of base knowledge about the leagues. There are also links to player biographies and team histories, all of which help make the Negro Leagues come to life decades after they faded away.

Another great source for information is BlackBaseball's site at *www.blackbaseball.com*. On the left side of the home page is a series of links, topped by a history link. There are also links to players and team histories.

This site also offers leads to further study of the subject, such as including a "Book of the Month" about Negro League baseball.

The All-American Girls Professional Baseball League

First, let's set a couple of things straight: Geena Davis, Rosie O'Donnell, and Madonna never played professional baseball. But their movie, *A League of Their Own*, cast a bright spotlight on the All-American Girls Professional Baseball League.

The league existed ever so briefly, starting in 1943 during World War II and ending in 1954. For a time, only the players took it seriously. But after a while, it developed a following.

Here's a capsulated look at a few sites that reflect that era in baseball history:

- **The First Ladies of Baseball**   This site (*members.aol.com/ legendlady/*) offers a history of the league and links to upcoming events, including a chance to meet some of the players who made the league a success.

- **The Girls of Summer**   This site (*www.exploratorium.edu/ baseball/girlsofsummer.html*) goes beyond the AAGPBL and highlights women's impact on baseball throughout its history. Biographies of important women in baseball history can be accessed through the "lineup card" on the right side of the page.

The First Ladies of Baseball site includes a history of the league.

- **AAGPBL Charm School Guide**   It's an awfully long address (*www.assumption.edu/HTML/Academic/history/ Hil13net/AAGPBL%20Charm%20School%20Guide/*) , but it's a lot of fun when you get there. This is the actual guide for appearance and manners that the women of the AAGPBL had to follow in order to be allowed to play.

Rounding the Bases

As we step on third and head for home in this history chapter, let's take a look at what we've covered. You should know by now:

- Where to go to begin your study of the history of the major leagues, whether you are looking for an obscure stat or an essay on the breaking of the color barrier.

- How to learn more about the Negro Leagues, their players, teams and the history in general.

- Where you can find information about the All-American Girls Professional Baseball League (other than in your local video store).

PART II

Sitting in the Bleachers

CHAPTER 4

Following the Major Leagues Online

Say what you want about Major League Baseball. Say the players make too much money. Say the owners make too much money and hold cities hostage for new stadiums. Say you were turned off by the strike a few years back.

But when it comes right down to it, you're still a fan. And who can blame you? For every contract dispute, there's a home-run race. For every stadium referendum, there's a no-hitter.

Whether you have a major-league team close enough to you to make regular trips to the ballpark possible or not, the major leagues are accessible to everyone today—that is, everyone with a computer. (And since you've got this book, I'm assuming that's you.)

There's more than enough information on the major leagues available on the Internet to satisfy even the most ardent baseball fan. In fact, there's enough information on the major leagues to make an entire book like this one.

Rather than give it all to you in this format, we're going to get you started, and let you do the rest on your own. This chapter is about national coverage of the major leagues—where to get the news, scores, and schedules for which you are looking.

We'll start this chapter with a look at baseball news. We'll cover the big boys—those major organizations that offer all the latest news on games, trades, signings, and more.

Next, we'll move on to the scoreboard and show you how you can follow all the action in progress. We'll even look at how you can use the Internet to literally listen to radio broadcasts of the games.

What You'll Learn in this Chapter:

▸ Where to find major-league news, including game coverage.

▸ How you can get up-to-the-minute updates on games in progress and even listen to games as they are played.

▸ Where you can find complete, season-long schedules, sorted by team and by date.

▸ Where you can find TV listings for national/regional coverage.

Then, we'll help you find out what's ahead with a look at sources for the major-league schedule. We'll conclude by showing you how you can plan your TV watching by using the Internet.

Finding the Baseball News on the Internet

More on That Later:

This entire section of the book is devoted to fans of Major League Baseball. The ensuing chapters cover more specific information on teams and players, where to find the statistical information you seek, and how to get involved in baseball chat with other fans.

Here's a little insider tidbit from the publishing industry: In order to get a book like this one out in time for the start of a baseball season, it has to be written during the offseason.

Okay, so maybe it's not the most earth-shattering news in the world. But you might think that writing about this topic during the offseason would make it harder to find the sites you're looking for. After all, the big baseball sites must shut down during the offseason, right?

Not so.

Just like your daily newspaper continues to cover baseball during the offseason, so do the Internet sites that cover the sport.

As any good baseball fan knows, what happens during the offseason often has more to do with how a team finishes a season than the outcome of games during the season. After all, it's during the offseason that teams are preparing their rosters for the coming year: signing free agents, making trades, even signing a manager or front-office personnel.

We've Already Seen...

You can find a lot of news at *www. majorleaguebaseball. com*, and at *www. totalbaseball.com*, in addition to the other sites we'll list here. But since we've already spent time there, we won't cover them in this section. We'll mention them later in the chapter, however.

All of that is baseball news, and all of it is available to you on the Internet. In fact, It's often available online before you can find it through another source. A player gets signed, and before you know it, there's a story available on the Web.

Let's take a look at some of the larger services that exist around the country to cover baseball at the major-league level.

The Entertainment and Sports Programming Network (that's ESPN)

It was touch-and-go there for a while, but ESPN ended up with the contract to telecast Major League Baseball games yet again. ESPN, the all-sports cable network, has long been a leader in sports television coverage. Since 1995, the network has also been a leader in online sports coverage, starting with ESPNET Sportszone.

Now, ESPN's Web site is part of the Go network. The address for the main baseball home page is *espn.go.com/mlb/index.html*. You can see it by checking out the following figure.

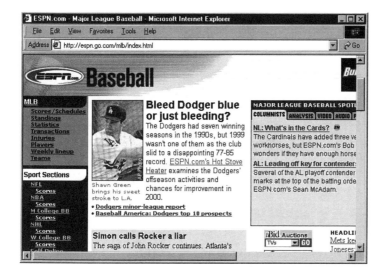

ESPN's baseball Web site is one of the most complete major-league sites available.

During the season, you'll find a lead sports story in the center of the page, usually centering on that day's action. During the offseason, it revolves around the biggest news of the day.

On the left side of the screen you'll find links to other baseball pages for everything from injury updates to schedules to transactions.

One thing that helps ESPN's baseball site stand out above most others is the link between the network and Major League Baseball. Because ESPN has the cable contract, it has a huge staff devoted to baseball coverage.

As such, you'll find commentary pieces from the likes of noted baseball writer/reporter Peter Gammons and other television personalities. And, ESPN does a great job of producing more than just coverage of the latest news by offering feature stories and in-depth coverage. In the figure above, the main story was about the Cincinnati Reds' plans for the offseason.

If you've never been to ESPN's site before, you'll probably find that it's hard to leave!

CBS Sportsline

Another television bigshot, CBS, also offers a great sports Web site called CBS Sportsline. Its baseball server can be reached at the following address: *cbs.sportsline.com/mlb/index.html*.

You can check it out in the following figure.

CBS Sportsline is a full-service Major League Baseball site.

Check the Local Sources:

Your local daily newspaper, especially if you are located in a major city that has a major-league franchise, might also offer a solid baseball Web service. Most newspapers offer pages of coverage of the local team, but some also devote staff hours to coverage of the league in general. They'll use a wire service such as the Associated Press to keep their pages updated. It's a good place to go for that local angle so many fans crave.

Like ESPN's site, if offers a main story in the center of the page, and links to supporting pages like standings, scores, and more. During the offseason and spring training, however, it offers one thing that the other sites don't.

It's called Fight For Jobs, and you can access from a link on the left side of the page. When you click on it, you go to the main Fight For Jobs page. Down the left side is a link to every major-league team. Just click on the team of your choice, and you'll get a baseball-diamond graphic with the players who are in the running for roster spots listed at their various positions. It's a great way to get a capsule look at the battles for spots on the major-league roster.

CBS Sportsline also offers a page called Player Salaries, which offers compensation information. If you're the least bit disillusioned with professional sports because of the amount of money the players are making, you might just want to avoid this page. It can be a little daunting.

USA Today

USA Today has a long-standing reputation for providing lots of news and sports in bite-size pieces. The Internet is perfect for relaying information in that format, and USA Today delivers.

USA Today's main baseball page can be found at *www.usatoday.com/sports/mlb.htm.*

You can see it in the following figure.

USA Today keeps you posted on the latest in baseball news.

Along with day-to-day coverage that USA Today's Web site offers, you also get the columns of the newspaper's long-time baseball writers, Mel Antonen and Rod Beaton. In addition to the online-only content, you can also read the print version of each day's sports section on the Web site.

USA Today also publishes an excellent weekly baseball magazine called Baseball Weekly. It has its own Web site at *www.usatoday.com/bbwfront.htm.*

Here, you can view much of the content of the magazine, which offers more in-depth coverage than the daily newspaper does.

Sports Pages Online

As almost everyone knows, nearly every newspaper of any size at all can be found on the Web. And finding the sports section in one of them isn't difficult: Just access your favorite search engine, punch in the name of the city...but wait, you need to know the name of the newspaper, right? Well, you can always just enter the name of the city, plus the word *newspaper*. But now it's getting a little messy. And even after you get to the front page, you still have to find the link to the sports section.

True, all this can be accomplished by an experienced surfer in less than a minute, but this is the 21st century! Who's got the time? Take the easy route, my friends, with Rich Johnson's Sportspages.com (*www.sportspages.com*). Just that one simple URL (short for Universal Resource Locator), and you'll arrive at a page with links to every notable sports section in the U.S. of A and Canada.

Since discovering Sportspages.com a few months ago, I've become addicted. I use it constantly for my work—it's amazing how much a little local color will add to a column. And I use it constantly as a fan, too. I live in Seattle, but my favorite sports teams are located in Kansas City and Minneapolis. Literally every day, I visit the newspapers in those cities—electronically, of course—for the latest on the Royals and Vikings. The site's not perfectly designed—why aren't the cities alphabetized?—but it's a little like my satellite dish...now that I've got it, I don't know how I ever managed without it.

Checking the Scores

This area has probably undergone more change and introduced baseball fans to more innovations than any other area of online baseball coverage.

Time was, of course, when a baseball fan had to sit with his (or her) ear to the radio to catch the latest scores. When the Internet came around, one of the things that surprised and pleased baseball fans was that they could see scores updated inning-by-inning as the games went along.

From there it went to push technology that allowed you to have a scrolling scoreboard on your desktop. But now, it's gone wild. You can listen to live radio broadcasts from all around the country. Or, you can *really* go nuts and follow the games, pitch-by-pitch, in full graphic detail on any of a number of Web sites.

They're Affiliated:
CBS Sportsline and Major League Baseball are partners in their online ventures. So when you access Baseball Live Plus through either site, you're going to the same place.

They've all got 'em:
In the previous section of this chapter, we covered baseball news. All of the sites we visited offer scoreboards of one type or another.

We could spend page after page after page covering how each of these services presents scores to its users, but I don't want to bore you with it.

You'll eventually find the ones you like best on your own. What I've done here is gone through them all for you, and picked out the ones that are a little different or offer a particular feature that others don't.

If you want to check out the latest and greatest in live baseball coverage on the Web, you need to go through Major League Baseball's site (*www.majorleaguebaseball.com*) or CBS Sportsline (*www.sportsline.com*).

Baseball Live Plus offers the latest innovation, 3D Pitch Tracker. It allows you to view each pitch of a major-league game, seeing the complete trajectory of the ball from the pitcher's hand to the bat or catcher's glove. To get there, click on the Scoreboard link from either the Sportsline or Major League Baseball site.

ESPN also offers pitch-by-pitch coverage through its scoreboard page; just click on the link from the main baseball page we visited above.

Don't need all that pizzazz? Try the Sporting News' Web site. It offers a complete scoreboard that is kept up-to-date, and also offers boxscores, a recap, and the pitching line. It doesn't offer all the extras, which is fine if all you need is the scores.

You can get to the scoreboard at *www.sportingnews.com/baseball/scoreboard/*.

Download Needed:
To use Baseball Live Plus, you need the Shockwave program from Macromedia, and 64MB of RAM, according to the site. This site also allows you to use RealAudio to listen to live broadcasts of major-league games.

Tired of These Yet?
If you're getting tired of seeing ESPN, CBS Sportsline and Major League Baseball, it's only because when it comes to baseball news and scores, they are the leaders. Spend some time ferreting around these sites, and you'll like what you find.

Total Baseball (*www.totalbaseball.com*) offers a feature called
TotalCast through its scoreboard page. You can see an example of
it in the following figure.

As you can see, for each batter there is a graphic that shows the
location of each pitch they faced. On the right is a text description
of the at-bat. You can also access quick stats about the player's
previous at-bats and season-long statistics. It'll make you feel like
you're in the announcer's booth.

*Total Baseball's
TotalCast offers
pitch-by-pitch cov-
erage.*

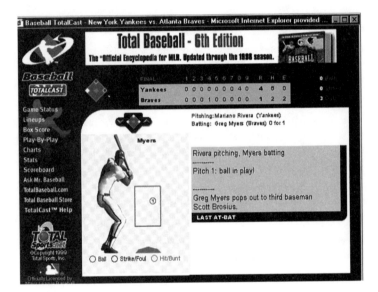

Reading the Schedule

Schedules aren't just for wallets and refrigerator magnets anymore.
Now, you can access them on the Web.

All of the big servers mentioned in this chapter have a schedule
area. Typically, they offer each day's schedule, available by
clicking on a date on a map.

This way, you can go back in time and see the results from any
day during the season. Or you can look ahead and see who your
favorite team is playing on a particular date.

Here are some good examples of schedules:

- ESPN's baseball site has a schedule you can access at *espn.go.com/today/sco.html*. You'll find today's scores there, and on the left side of the screen will be the current month in view. You can go forward or backward in time using the appropriate arrows above the calendar.

- CBS Sportsline's schedule page is at *www.sportsline.com/ u/baseball/mlb/sched.htm*. Click the Daily Schedules button and you'll see a menu that offers you the chance to pick a month. Once you've done that, you can pick a date.

- If you want to go to a particular team's schedule, go to their official Web page. They all have schedules. Or, you can visit the page ESPN maintains for each team. On the main ESPN baseball page, open the pull-down menu called Teams and select your team. When you get to the team's page, click the schedule link.

Checking the TV Listings

So, with all this live coverage on the Web you still want to watch the games on television?

Well, you can check out ESPN's TV listings at *espn.go.com/ tvlistings/index.html*.

If you are looking for a game that is on local television, you can check out the appropriate station's Web site and peruse its listings.

Or, you can visit your favorite team's Web site. They often post the television schedule on their site.

Rounding the Bases

In this chapter, we've looked at what the big-time baseball outlets on the Web have to offer in the form of baseball news and basic information like scores. By now, you have learned:

- Where you can find baseball news on the Web, including in-season game coverage, feature stories, columnists, and offseason news.

- How to follow the action during a game by using a score-board.

- How to follow live action using a specialized scoreboard that offers pitch-by-pitch coverage.

- Where to look for schedules for all of Major League Baseball and for your favorite teams.

- Where to find TV listings so you can watch the games while you surf the Web!

CHAPTER 5

Finding Your Favorite Team or Player Online

Everybody has at least one favorite team. For some people, it's whoever happens to be winning that particular season. But even in that case, it's still a favorite team—it just happens to change every year.

Whether your favorite team is the long-suffering Cubs, the ever-mighty Yankees, or an up-and-down team like the Cincinnati Reds, you love them. You rejoice in their accomplishments and suffer with their defeats. But you're always with them.

Being a fan used to mean reading the daily paper, listening to the games on the radio, watching them on television, and attending as many as possible in person. Today, we've got another option, the Internet.

With the Web, you can keep up-to-date on everything about your team through its official site and many other not-so-official sites.

So, whether you want to rant with other fans about how that big-dollar free agent has turned into a bum or buy box seats for the next game, you can get it done online, around the clock.

What's your pleasure? Do you want to read the official line coming straight from the team's public relations office? Do you want to read opinions from professional baseball writers who are covering the games? Do you want to hear what the average man on the street thinks? Do you want to offer your own opinion?

Regardless, you can do it all online. There are a number of different types of sites that you can find on the Internet to help you follow your team.

First, there are the official team sites, the ones that are run by the franchises themselves or Major League Baseball. Then there are

What You'll Learn in This Chapter:

▶ The team-sponsored sites, and what they have to offer to the devoted fan.

▶ The team pages on the big sports services, and how they differ from the others.

▶ The team coverage pages you can find from local media outlets.

▶ The fan-created pages and some of the wild stuff you can find there.

▶ The official and unofficial sites devoted to various players in the major leagues.

the sites (sometimes called "clubhouses") that are part of major sports services like ESPN, CBS Sportsline, and the Sporting News. Then, there are the sites that are run by local newsgathering organizations, like all-sports radio stations and daily newspapers. Finally, there are the sites created by the fans themselves, ranging from hero-worship to a team's worst nightmare. In this chapter, we'll take a look at all of them.

Official Team Sites

Depending on your definition of the word "official," every major-league team has either one or two official sites. Each team has its own site, with its own address, run by the team itself and billed as, for example, "The Official Online Home of the..."

As members of Major League Baseball, however, each team also has a site that is part of the major leagues' site at *www. majorleaguebaseball.com.*

Let's take a look at some examples and you'll see the difference clearly.

Team-sponsored Sites

Go to your favorite search engine and do a search based on your favorite team's name. What you'll find may amaze you.

Most teams have at least 20 different Web sites devoted to them in the various categories I covered in the chapter introduction. Hidden somewhere in there is the one, true "official" team site—the one that is sponsored by the team itself.

To make life easier for you, I've compiled the list of official sites for the 30 teams in the major leagues.

Beware the Word "Official":

On the World Wide Web, the word "official" gets tossed about rather loosely. Any Joe can create a site about the Florida Marlins, for example, and call it the "official site" of the Marlins. For the most part, search engines do a pretty good job of indicating which sites are official and which are not. If you have any questions, however, check out the copyright at the bottom of the home page for the site.

Major League Team	Web-site address
Anaheim Angels	*www.angelsbaseball.com*
Arizona Diamondbacks	*www.azdiamondbacks.com*
Atlanta Braves	*www.atlantabraves.com*
Baltimore Orioles	*www.theorioles.com*
Boston Red Sox	*www.redsox.com*
Chicago Cubs	*www.cubs.com*
Chicago White Sox	*www.chisox.com*
Cincinnati Reds	*www.cincinnatireds.com*

Major League Team	Web-site address
Cleveland Indians	www.indians.com
Colorado Rockies	www.coloradorockies.com
Detroit Tigers	www.detroittigers.com
Florida Marlins	www.flamarlins.com
Houston Astros	www.astros.com
Kansas City Royals	www.kcroyals.com
Los Angeles Dodgers	www.dodgers.com
Milwaukee Brewers	www.milwaukeebrewers.com
Minnesota Twins	www.mntwins.com
Montreal Expos	www.montrealexpos.com
New York Mets	www.mets.com
New York Yankees	www.yankees.com
Oakland Athletics	www.oaklandathletics.com
Philadelphia Phillies	www.phillies.com
Pittsburgh Pirates	www.pirateball.com
San Diego Padres	www.padres.com
San Francisco Giants	www.sfgiants.com
Seattle Mariners	www.mariners.org
St. Louis Cardinals	www.stlcardinals.com
Tampa Bay Devil Rays	www.devilrays.com
Texas Rangers	www.texasrangers.com
Toronto Blue Jays	www.bluejays.ca

While they run the gamut from conservative to flamboyant in terms of design, they tend to offer similar information. Typically, you'll find a complete roster, schedule and statistics for the team. You'll get a recap of the most recent game. You'll also be able to hear clips from radio broadcasts.

Sometimes You Can Get the Scoop:

During the 1999 playoffs and World Series, rumors swirled that Atlanta Braves hitting coach Don Baylor would be named the Chicago Cubs' new manager once the World Series was over.

If you were Internet-savvy, however, you didn't need to listen to rumors. The Cubs' own Web site had an announcement of Baylor as the new manager more than a week before the "official" announcement was made!

Some also offer a history section, some offer video, and some offer live chats with players and front-office executives.

Since the team sponsors the site, you'll also get other news, such as community involvement, about the organization. Usually, there's a minor-league report as well. And, most important (to the team, that is), there are pages where you can order tickets or team merchandise.

A good example is the Texas Rangers home page at *www. texasrangers.com*. You can see it in the following figure.

The Texas Rangers' official site is a complete resource for fans.

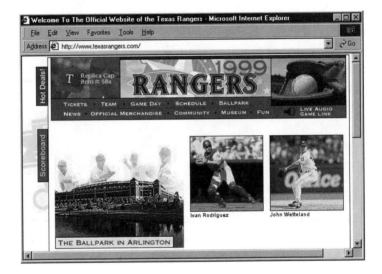

One advantage to the official site over another site is that some items of interest to fans—such as the new uniforms announced on the Rangers' site—might not be found elsewhere.

But the key difference is that each of these team-sponsored Web sites is unique. The team "clubhouse" pages you find on other sites are going to be identical from team to team.

Major League Baseball's Team Pages

The other source for "official" team pages is Major League Baseball. It's a site we've visited many times before.

The site, *www.majorleaguebaseball.com*, offers a team page for each of the 30 teams in the majors. There, you'll find information on past games and the schedule for the season, bios on the players

and manager, plus spring training and minor league information.
Let's take a look at the Detroit Tigers' schedule for the 2000
season.

1. Go to the Major League Baseball home page at the address
   listed above.

2. From the drop-down "Clubs" menu at the left, select Detroit
   Tigers.

3. In the menu on the left of the Tigers page, click on Schedule.
   You'll get a complete list of games for the season.

▼ Try It Yourself

It's a nice interactive schedule. For games already played, you can
click on the game and get a boxscore and game summary, making
it a nice archive for fans.

Team Sites on Sports Servers

Just about all the major sports services on the Internet offer a
team or "clubhouse" page for every team in the major leagues.
Their format varies based on the provider, but a few things are
consistent.

You're going to find results, boxscores, game summaries, standings, statistics, and so on. You might find an injury report or a list
of player salaries.

ESPN offers a notes column that includes the latest news from
each of the major-league teams. Let's use them as an example.

To get to ESPN's team index, you can use the following URL
address: *http://espn.go.com/mlb/clubhouses/index.html.* Or, you
can go to ESPN's main home page, click on the Baseball link,
then click on the Teams link.

Once you're at the index page, click the name of the team of your
choice. Below you can see the St. Louis Cardinals team page.

On the main page, you can see ESPN's notes column, chock full
of news and tidbits about the Cardinals.

Of course, there are many services that offer baseball team pages.
You'll find them from CBS Sportsline (*www.sportsline.com*), the
Sporting News (*www.thesportingnews.com*), Total Baseball

Player "Pages":
Any of these team
sites, or clubhouse
pages, will have
information about
particular players, as
well. It ranges from
mere statistics to
complete biogra-
phies and year-by-
year highlights like
you might find in a
team's media guide.
So if you're looking
for information on
your favorite player,
you might want to
check out one of
these team pages,
go to the roster, and
click on the link to
the player's name.

(*www.totalbaseball.com*), and Fox Sports (*http://foxsports.com*). There are many others as well.

ESPN's clubhouse page for the Cardinals includes a news update on the team.

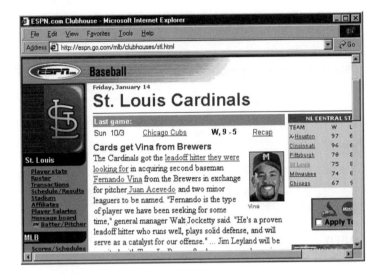

Coverage on Local Media Outlets

The most thorough coverage of your local baseball franchise is probably going to come from a local media outlet, such as a daily newspaper, all-sports radio station or cable television channel.

In some cases, a media outlet such as a daily newspaper will maintain an actual page for a particular team. But at the very least, you're going to get outstanding coverage of the team—a chance to read the latest stories that have been in the paper and more. That's particularly useful for people who are away from home but want to keep up with their favorite teams. (Or, if you happen to live in a different city than the one in which your team plays.)

You can access the local site and find the information you want. Let's take a look at a couple of examples.

The San Francisco Examiner

The sports staff at the San Francisco Examiner newspaper is a busy group. They cover all the sports teams in the Bay Area, which is quite a list indeed. In baseball, of course, that means the San Francisco Giants and the Oakland Athletics.

To get to the Examiner's coverage of these teams, go to *http://examiner.com/sports/*. That's the Examiner's main sports page. If you scroll down the page, you'll come to a menu called, "Local Teams," which has links to Giants and A's coverage.

Click on the link to Giants, and you get a page like the one you see in the following figure.

Coverage of the Giants offered by the San Francisco Examiner.

More Baseball News:

In case you're skipping around in this book—and shame on you if you are—Chapter 4, "Finding the Major Leagues Online," offers more information about news coverage of Major League Baseball.

In the middle of the page is links to the latest stories that have appeared in the newspaper about the Giants. But across the top of the screen, you can see links to team-page information like statistics, the roster, results, etc.

WCCO's Channel 4000

Right here in frigid Minnesota, a local television station is a leader in online content. The television station, WCCO, is joined by its partner on the radio, also WCCO, which carries the Minnesota Twins games. Their Web site, "Channel 4000," has a Twins home page at *www.wcco.com/sports/twins/*. You can see it in the following figure.

Because of the partnership between these media outlets and the team, you're not going to find a lot of harsh criticism of the team. But there's plenty here for the serious fan, and it's an example of local media offering a team page (and a good one).

*You can follow
the Twins at this
local TV/radio sta-
tion's Web site.*

Fan-created Team and Player Sites

**One Man's
Opinion:**

You can also have a
great time with
sites devoted to the
hatred of a particu-
lar team. Teams
that fans love to
hate, like the
Yankees, often have
sites created by
people who dislike
them intensely.
They can get a little
raunchy, but most
of the time they're
good, clean fun.

As I said earlier in this chapter, any Joe can create a Web site
about a team and call it "official." Even more Joes can create Web
sites about a team and *not* call them official, and that's the beauty
of it.

If you have some free time some day, take a look at some of the
fan-created Web sites about your favorite team (or any team, for
that matter). They offer everything from unabashed worship to
some of the harshest, below-the-belt cheap shots any good fan can
offer.

How do you find them? Let's walk through an example of a
search for a fan-based Web site. Just for the fun of it, let's look
for sites about one of the majors' oldest teams, the Chicago Cubs.

Try It Yourself ▼

1. Go to the Yahoo! search engine at *www.yahoo.com.*

2. In the Search box, type Chicago Cubs, and click the Search
   button.

3. Under Category Matches, click on the link to Chicago Cubs.

4. On the next screen, click on the link to Fan Pages. You will
   get a list of Fan Pages from which to choose. Happy surfing!

▲

There are several great fan-created pages about the Cubs. One of them is called the Miserable Cubs Fan Forum, located at *www.geocities.com/Colosseum/Track/7004/*. You can see it in the following figure.

The Miserable Cubs Fan Forum offers fans a chance to sound off.

This one's a little tough on the home team, but it offers fans a chance to give their opinions about various Cubs-related topics in the Issue of the Week section. It's worth visiting.

Individual Players' Sites

You want to pay homage to your favorite player? Visit a site devoted just to him. No, not one of those biography-and-stats sites that the team pages offer—I mean a site that's devoted just to a particular player.

Fans often create these sites, and they range from ones that young female fans have created because a particular player is "cute" to sites that honor a player's contribution to a franchise over time.

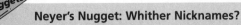

Neyer's Nugget: Whither Nicknames?

Labor issues notwithstanding, I would argue that the great majority of things relating to baseball are better than ever. The hitters are stronger, the pitchers throw harder, the fielders are more spectacular. With a satellite dish, you can watch 35 games per week. With a computer, you can follow *every* game, pitch by pitch, as they're thrown (and if you're smart, your boss will never suspect a thing).

There is, however, one aspect of baseball that has been in serious decline for some time now: nicknames. Lou Gehrig had three nicknames: Columbia Lou, Biscuit Pants, and (of course) The Iron Horse. Ted Williams boasted no fewer than *four* monikers: The Kid, Teddy Ballgame, The Thumper, and The Splendid Splinter.

Now look at two of today's biggest stars: Ken Griffey (Junior) and Mark McGwire (Big Mac). Each has only one nickname, and neither of those nicknames is particularly colorful. Why the change? Because in the old days, sportswriters considered the invention and dissemination of nicknames among their job duties, and they don't any more. Fortunately, there is hope, in the form of Web sites devoted to teams and run by fans. One of the best of these sites is Kev & Scott's Astros Connection (*www.astrosconnection.com*), where Kev and Scott, plus a number of helpers, discuss anything and everything relating to the Astros. But what's important in our current discussion is the Kev & Scott Glossary of Terms (*www.astrosconnection.com/html/glossary.html*), in which we find solid, (mostly) fan-invented nicknames for various Astros and non-Astros, including ex-Astros first baseman Glenn Davis (The Big Bopper), ex-Astros pitcher Danny Darwin (Dr. Death), ex-Astros outfielder Carl Everett (The Demolition Man), Padres first baseman Ryan Klesko (Donut Truck), and current Astros pitcher Scott Elarton (The Outlaw). Their best, however, is the nickname for the always-dirty Craig Biggio: Pig-Pen.

Nicknames will never be what they once were, but Web-savvy fans won't give up without a tough fight.

Some of them are actual "official" sites that are created by the
player (more likely by their agent or management group). Some
players even have sites that highlight their careers but are actually
set up to benefit a charity of their choice.

Cal Ripken, Jr., holder of the major-league record for consecutive
games played, ended the 1999 season just nine hits short of 3,000
for his career. He's one of the players who has his own official
Web site. His domain name is the number of games he played to
break Lou Gehrig's record: *www.2131.com*. You can see it in the
figure below.

The site includes day-by-day coverage of Ripken's on-field
exploits, but the Out of Uniform link also details his work in the
community and other off-field involvements. It's a great example
of a player's page.

*Cal Ripken, Jr.'s
official home
page.*

If you want to see some fan-created player pages, just do a search
for the player's name, and you'll get them. If it's reliable information about a player you seek, then go to one of the team pages
covered earlier in this chapter.

Rounding the Bases

Now you know where to look for information about your favorite
team or player. In this chapter, we covered:

- Finding official team Web sites and the team pages created
  by Major League Baseball.

- Where to look for team clubhouses created by major sports
  servers like ESPN.

- How local media outlets present information about teams on
  the Web.

- Some examples of fan-created Web pages about teams and
  players.

- How major-league players portray themselves on the Internet,
  and how their fans do it as well.

CHAPTER 6

Stats, Stats, and More Stats

More than any other major sport, baseball is a game of stats. It starts with runs, hits, and errors and goes all the way through batting average, earned run average, and more. Beyond all that are the "designer" stats that have come into being in the last decade or so—stats created by baseball fans and historians in an effort to determine a player's true value to his team.

Bill James, author of the *Baseball Abstract* book that took statistics to a new level has "invented" a stat called Runs Created that attempts to measure a player's overall offensive value to his team.

Why?

It's a good question. The answer might be this: While stats are cold, hard facts, they can be manipulated to argue virtually any point. For example, one typical argument is whether it's better for a team to have an outstanding leadoff hitter who steals bases or a big-time slugger who belts homers. The leadoff man sets the table and starts the rallies, the home run hitter drives in three or four runs with one swing of the bat. Who's more important to a successful team?

Statisticians and baseball fanatics have attempted to prove over the years through use of statistics the answer to that question. It's been the catalyst behind the creation of new units of measure in baseball and the fodder for—believe it or not—numerous studies conducted at major universities around the country.

But what if you just want to keep track of who's leading the league in homers, doubles, wins, and strikeouts—the basic stats?

In this chapter, we'll cover the gamut of statistics on the Internet. There are countless sources of the basic statistics of everyday baseball, and we'll take a look at a few of those. We'll also look at a source or two for statistics for years gone by.

What You'll Learn in This Chapter:

- ▶ Day-to-day statistics page on major baseball servers on the Web.
- ▶ In-depth statistics for baseball fans like daily leaders.
- ▶ Other statistics resources like historical stats.
- ▶ Research into and about baseball statistics.
- ▶ Unusual statistics that attempt to measure player performance in new ways.

Then, we'll look at some of the more arcane statistics that can be, or have been, created for and by baseball fans. And, we'll look at some theories on statistics and how they can be interpreted to which you may or may not want to subscribe.

Day-to-Day Statistics

The starting point for most baseball fans is the day-to-day statistics that help make the game more interesting. The statement, "Randy Johnson pitched a shutout last night," will almost certainly lead to this question: "How many strikeouts did he have?"

Only the most basic baseball fan (and that certainly can't be you) finds that the final score of any game is enough. Imagine this description of an Atlanta Braves victory: "The Braves beat the Astros 3-0 last night. Greg Maddux was dominant on the mound, and some fine offensive plays by Chipper Jones helped produced the runs the Braves needed."

Huh?

Any self-respecting baseball fan is going to want to know how many innings Maddux pitched and how many hits he gave up, at the very least. And, they'll probably want to know how many hits Jones had and if he had any homers or how many runs he drove in.

Ah, statistics.

By the Way:

Stats freaks are often also interested in fantasy sports. For those of you who are, we haven't forgotten about you. You can use this chapter to help gather information for use in a fantasy league, then read chapters 11 and 12, which are both about fantasy baseball leagues.

The daily newspaper is full of boxscores, and the average fan's craving for more and more data has forced those boxes to get bigger every year. It used to be simple at-bats, runs, hits, and RBI for hitters. In many large papers, it now includes strikeouts and walks, runners left on base and more for every player in every game. Then, usually once a week, the paper will print the stats for every player in the major leagues.

On the Internet, you can get that every day, 24 hours a day.

Any of the major servers we've covered in other chapters—Major League Baseball's, ESPN's, CBS Sportsline's, and many, many more—will offer you daily boxscores and complete statistics for each team in the majors.

There's really no need for us to cover all of that here. So let's take a look at some of the more out-of-the-ordinary services that some of these statistics servers offer.

Neyer's Nugget: Where to Go Online for Stats

Every day in my work—actually, most people don't think that what I do is "work," and most days I think they're right—I use statistics. And even if I didn't "work," I would still use statistics every day. There are three Web sites that give me just about everything that I need, whether I'm working or not.

When I am working, I write a daily baseball column for ESPN.com, so naturally *www.espn.com* is my first stop when looking for stats. And as Bob Temple has already mentioned, ESPN.com's statistical coverage is excellent. But nobody's perfect, and if I'm looking for something and I can't find it at "home," a trip to CNNSI.com (*www.cnnsi.com*) often does the trick. Although CNNSI.com's editorial content is no better than their top competitors, they've built a fine statistical package that includes sortable team stats for the current season, active leaders in primary statistics, and the career records for every man who ever played major league baseball.

If you're looking for non-traditional stats, what practitioners call *sabermetrics*, I recommend the Baseball Prospectus Web site at *www.baseballprospectus.com*. The Baseball Prospectus is actually an annual book, perhaps the most worthy successor to Bill James's late, lamented *Baseball Abstract*. But during the season, the book's authors also generate a wealth of new content, including the most intelligent transaction analyses you'll find anywhere. The BP crew has devoted itself to answering some of baseball's longest-running questions: How much work for a young pitcher is too much? How can we accurately evaluate fielding skill? How much influence does a catcher have on his pitchers? The bonus here is that you can watch it all happen at their Web site.

Finally, it's important to remember that the Internet is a fast-changing medium. What's not there today might be there tomorrow, and vice versa. At this writing, ESPN.com and CNNSI.com are the best sources for statistics. But every once in a while, you should check out the other big sites, too, because you never know what's new until you look.

Sortable Stats from Major League Baseball

Heck, anybody can give you B.J. Surhoff's batting average at any given moment. In fact, most boxscores in daily papers across the country report each player's batting average every day.

But did you know that Surhoff led the American League in at-bats in 1999? You may not care, but you're about to find out just how easy it is to find interesting facts like that on the Internet.

Major League Baseball's Web site offers what it calls "Sortable Stats" that allow you to use any major statistical category to sort the list of players. You already know that Surhoff led the American League in at-bats in 1999, but who leads the majors now, as you read this book?

Try It Yourself ▼

1. Go to the Major League Baseball Web site at *www.majorleaguebaseball.com*.

2. Click on the Stats button on the left side of the home page. You will be taken to the Sortable Stats page.

3. Under the American League list, click on Player Sortables (YTD). It defaults to a list of American League players, sorted by the Home Run category, as you can see in the following figure.

4. Next to Batters, click All. In Select League, click MLB. You'll have a list of all major-league players, but still sorted by Home Runs.

5. Click the AB category, and the list will re-display, sorted by at-bats leaders.

▲

Since I did this sort during the offseason, it gave me the results for the completed 1999 season, showing that Neifi Perez of the Colorado Rockies led the majors in at-bats. If you do it during the season, it will show you the year-to-date leader.

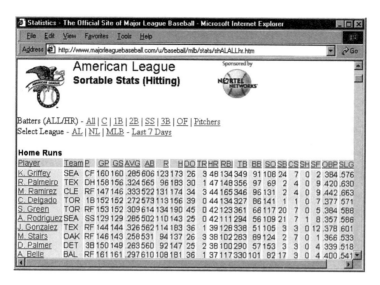

Sortable Stats allows you to query any statistical category.

As you could see from the category headers, you can sort any of the lists by position and include only information for the last seven days if you wish. That way you could, for example, find out which National League pitcher had the most strikeouts in the past seven days.

Daily Leaders from ESPN

ESPN's services also offers a form of sortable stats. But beyond that, ESPN offers lists of leaders for each day of the major-league season.

Let's say, for the sake of argument, you would like to know who led the major leagues in stolen bases yesterday. Why you would need to know this, I don't know, but let's just say you do!

Head to the ESPN Web site at *http://espn.go.com*. Click your way through to the baseball statistics page. (You can also simply go there directly by way of *http://espn.go.com/mlb/statistics/index.html*.)

You can see the page in the following figure.

One Man's Opinion:

The last-seven-days sort is particularly valuable for the fantasy-league owner who needs to make a roster move. If your team is lacking in home runs, for example, you can use that sort to find out who the hottest home-run hitters are, thus allowing you to pick up a streaking player.

*Find out who the
daily leaders are
at ESPN's Web
site.*

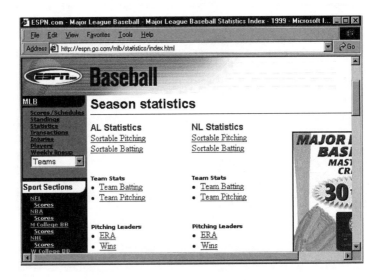

Scroll down the page to the Daily Leaders section, and click on
the Stolen Bases link. You'll get a list of the leaders in stolen
bases for the previous day's play, separated by league.

Team-by-Team Statistics for Decades Past

There are many sources for yesterday's stats or even the stats for
the season-to-date. Let's take a look at a source for stats from
years gone by.

The Major League Baseball Statistics page at
http://statsc.freeservers.com/mlb_index.html offers historical team
stats and individual player statistics for the 1970s, '80s, and '90s.

Clicking on any team's History link will show you their record
for every year since 1970, including the manager's name.

Clicking on the link to any decade takes you to year-by-year individual statistics for every player on each team. Want to know what
Rod Carew hit for the Angels in 1980? Click on the 1980–89 link
for the Angels and you'll find that in 1980, Carew hit .331.

Unusual or Newly-Created Statistics

Earlier in this chapter, we discussed the Runs Created statistic that
has come into play in recent years. There are others, like Total
Average, that have combined various "regular" statistics into a formula that—the creators believe—accurately depicts something or
another.

It's all designed so that we can settle arguments on such lofty topics as, is it better to have a great closer or a great starting pitcher?

Let's take a look at some of these statistical analyses and see what you think of them.

The High Boskage House

The High Boskage House describes itself as a side-line for a regular business, yet it updates its theoretical statistics daily throughout the major-league season.

The HBH believes that its formula can predict with breathtaking accuracy the ability of a given player to impact his team's runs scored and/or runs allowed total.

What drags this site down is the tedious explanations of how these results are produced. That is, of course, unless you are into that sort of thing, in which case you'll probably find it interesting.

The site (*www.highboskage.com*) goes into great detail to explain how its theory works, then offers up-to-date statistical listings to prove its point (see the following figure).

In reality, though, it's fascinating reading. Spend some time bouncing around this site to learn more about the theory, and you'll like what you find.

By the Way:
Some of the stats you hear bandied about truly mean nothing. The ones I've chosen to list here have clearly involved a lot of research and testing over years of statistics to develop a theory.

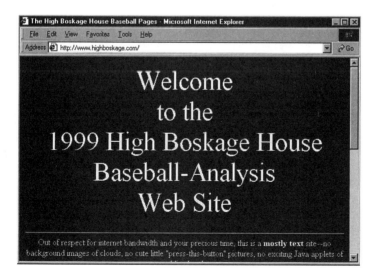

The High Boskage House keeps its stats updated daily.

Estimated Runs Produced

Part of the Baseball Stuff site (*www.baseballstuff.com*) is an essay
on a statistic called Estimated Runs Produced. It's written by a
man named Paul Johnson. It differs from Bill James' Runs
Created formula, yet it has received James' endorsement.

The theory attempts to prove an individual players' ability to produce runs for his team, much like James' theory. It just claims to
do a better job of it.

I suggest you read the essay at *www.baseballstuff.com/btf/pages/
essays/jameserp.htm*. It's interesting reading.

UC-Berkeley Research That's Better Than Magic Numbers

As the baseball seasons turn from the dog days of August into
serious pennant and wild-card races in September, baseball fans
start to talk about their team's magic number.

The magic number is simple to understand: It's the number of
games that the leading team must win or its nearest competitor
must lose in order for the team to clinch a division title or playoff
berth. In other words, if the Yankees are in first place, the Red
Sox are in second, and the Yankees' magic number is three, then
any combination of Yankee wins and Red Sox losses equaling
three clinches the division title for New York.

Well, leave it to the minds at the University of California-
Berkeley to come up with a "better" way of determining what a
team needs to do to reach the playoffs. They show how many
games a team must win in order to clinch a playoff berth or a
division title.

They go the other way, too, and offer a statistic that shows how
many games a team must avoid losing in order to avoid being
eliminated from the playoffs.

The site can be seen in the following figure. The address is
http://riot.ieor.Berkeley.edu/~baseball/.

At UC-Berkeley, they believe their formula is better than the magic number.

Just click on either the American League or National League logo, and you'll get the complete standings, up-to-date. You'll be able to know how many games your team needs to win in order to be playoff-bound.

By the Way:
This research has been conducted by RIOT, which stands for Remote Inter-active Optimization Testbed, whatever that means.

More Statistical Analysis

There's a lot more statistical analysis available on the Internet. Here's a quick look at a couple of resources for you to consider:

- **Society for American Baseball Research**   SABR is a member organization that's open to baseball fans—SERIOUS baseball fans—from around the world. SABR was founded by a group of "statistorians," baseball lovers who combine history with statistics to study the game. The Web site is located at *www.sabr.org*.

- **Stathead Consulting**   This site claims to be the Internet's most complete free baseball research library. It offers its own performance ratings for hitters and pitchers. The site is located at *www.stathead.com*.

- **Thinking Baseball**   This site offers articles, a daily update and even trade analysis. Rather than presenting stats, it analyzes moves that teams have made using statistics as a basis. The site can be found at *www.thinkingbaseball.com*.

Rounding the Bases

If the information presented in this chapter doesn't include
enough statistics sources for you, then you really are a stats nut.

We covered:

- "Regular" statistics sources on the Web and some of the
  "irregular" statistics offerings they have for you.

- Where you can find information about some of the more
  unusual stats that researchers have developed over the years.

- How people are using statistical formulas to prove everything
  from who's better than whom to what teams need to do to
  reach the playoffs.

- Where you can find organizations that are dedicated to study-
  ing statistics and using them to analyze teams and players.

CHAPTER 7

Talkin' Baseball—The Hot Stove League

For the last three chapters, you've learned where to find the information you seek about Major League Baseball. If you were already a big fan, that information no doubt helped turn you into a fanatic. If you were just a casual fan, finding out what the Internet has to offer can only increase your love of the game.

Unless you're a hermit, however, it isn't much fun to be a baseball fan alone. It's much more enjoyable when you can share that love with other people.

That can mean sitting in front of a big screen with some buddies and watching the games, arguing over the games at the local tavern, or taking your kids out to the ol' ball yard.

The Internet, of course, offers you more ways to share your love of—or interest in—the game with others. You can even use your love for the game to make *new* friends!

Chat rooms, bulletin boards, and mailing lists are the most popular ways to interact with other users of the Internet who are baseball fans.

In this chapter, we will look at all three of those offerings on the Internet.

We'll start with chat rooms, which have become increasingly popular on the Internet. We'll move on the bulletin boards, also called message boards or newsgroups.

Finally, we'll look at mailing lists. We'll look at the differences between each type of Internet "talk," and give some examples as to where you can find them.

What You'll Learn in This Chapter:

▶ How chat rooms allow baseball fans to talk to each other live.

▶ Where you can typically find chat rooms full of baseball fans.

▶ The different types of bulletin boards and how they work.

▶ A complete list of USENET newsgroups about Major League Baseball.

▶ How mailing lists work, and how baseball fans use them.

By the Way:
This chapter covers mailing lists, bulletin boards, and chat rooms on the Internet. It doesn't however, cover such activities on other services like America Online. We've devoted an entire chapter to AOL's baseball offerings: Chapter 18, "Baseball on AOL."

Baseball Chat

When people think of chat rooms, most probably think about America Online. The truth is that chatting on the Internet has been every bit as popular as chatting on America Online, but AOL has brought it into the mainstream, so to speak.

Some people might think that chatting is just for those who want to make a "love connection" of one type or another on the Internet. Again, the truth is much better than the myth.

Chatting on the Internet covers the complete gamut of topics that Web sites do. If you can find a topic on the Internet, chances are good you can find chat areas associated with it, as well. Baseball is no exception.

There are lots of places you can get involved in baseball chat on the Internet. In fact, many of the sites we've already covered in this book have chat areas associated with them.

Typically, all you need to do is look for a Chat button or link, and you'll be taken to a chat area within the site you're visiting. In this chapter, though, we're going to look at a few areas that we haven't seen before.

Just What Are Chat Rooms, Anyway?

Think of chat rooms as telephone calls without the crimp in your neck (you might get a crimp in your fingers, however).

A chat room is an area online (a Web page, for example) in which you are connected live to other users of the same page. You type in a message, click a button, and the message appears on, your screen and the screens of anyone else who is visiting that chat "room" at the same time. When someone else posts a message, you see it instantly, too.

Usually, each person in the room has chosen a "screen name" to use in the room. Your messages will appear on-screen following your screen name. For example, if you chose the screen name "baseball nut" and you typed the message, "Red Sox rule," it would probably look like this:

"Baseball nut: Red Sox rule"

Sometimes, chat rooms can get out of hand. If you've got, say, a dozen people in a chat room, all "talking" at the same time, it can get really confusing to follow the conversation. By the time you respond to one person, five or six other messages may have been posted. But it can be very fun and exciting, too.

Let's take a look at a couple of different chat rooms and how they work on the Internet.

Chatting on MLBFan.com

MLBFan.com is a site that claims to be "for the fans, by the fans." It offers a chat rooms for baseball fans.

You can see the MLBFan.com site in the following figure.

MLBFan.com offers major-league fans the chance to talk to one another.

By the Way:
Keep the language clean, and try not to set off World War III in your chat discussions. It's one thing to disagree, it's another to get insulting.

At this writing, MLBFan.com was in the process of completely re-doing its site for the first season of the new millennium. The chat area was expected to be up and running before the start of the 2000 regular season.

Baseball Chat!

Another chat area you might want to take a peek at is Baseball Chat!

You can get there by going to the following Web address: *www.4-lane.com/sportschat/newsc/bb_index.html.* You can see it in the following figure.

This site is a little more straightforward in the way you use it. Just scroll down the page and enter a name you would like to use for your chat, click the Get in Sports Chat window, and you're there.

By the Way:
Occasionally, you might come across a site in which you are asked to "join" or "become a member" of the site in order to enter a chat room. Most of the time, you can join these sites without cost. Sometimes, however, there is a fee to be paid to be a member.

*Baseball Chat! is
another good
chat area for fans.*

Bulletin Boards, Newsgroups, and Message Boards

The heading for this section of the chapter is a little deceiving. Generally speaking, bulletin boards, newsgroups and message boards are one and the same.

However, if you want to get technical about it, there are some subtle differences between the "boards" and newsgroups.

In either case, however, the idea is that you find a subject area of your liking, and you post a message to it that other people can read.

By the Way:

Typically, when you post a message it stays up for a specified period of time, such as a week or a month. After that, it disappears. Each bulletin board is different, however, and the rules vary.

The key difference between this type of communication and chat is that while chat is live, bulletin boards are not. It's just like a cork bulletin board up on a wall. You can tack a message up and it stays there for other people to read whenever they want to.

There are even more bulletin boards on the Internet than there are chat rooms. Most of your major baseball services offer a button or link called Boards or Post a Message or the like for you to use to share opinions with other baseball fans.

Baseball Bulletin Boards

You can't get a much better name for a Web site devoted to baseball bulletin boards than Baseball Boards. You can check out the site at *www.baseballboards.com.*

Baseball Boards maintains bulletin boards in six major categories: Major League Baseball, Business of Baseball, Trade Rumors, Stats, Minors and Prospects, and Collecting. But it goes well beyond that—there's also a bulletin board for every team in the Major Leagues.

Some of these boards are "moderated." That is, there is a real human being in charge of watching over the board to make sure that the conversation stays focused and doesn't get out of control.

If you want to get a picture of the entire list of boards they offer, just click View the Detailed List of Baseball Boards link, and you'll see them all.

Just click the link to the topic of your choice, and you'll be there in no time. For example, if you wanted to get into the board for the Baltimore Orioles, you would click on the link to Orioles. You would see a page that looks like the following figure.

One Man's Opinion:

What's so impressive about this site is not only the vast number of boards and topics that are offered, but how active it is. Even in the middle of the offseason, when you pick a topic, you'll see posts made very recently. This site doesn't appear to take any time off.

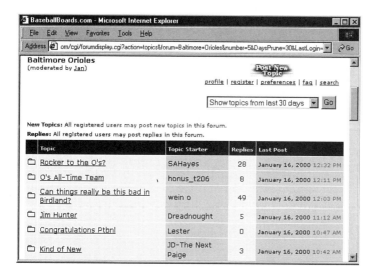

Baseball Boards offers bulletin boards for every major league team.

As you can see, there's a list of topics that have been discussed about the Orioles. To read any of the lists of messages, all you have to do it click the topic name, which is a link.

If you want to start a new topic, go to the very bottom of the list of topics, and click the link called Post New Topic.

Once you've read the messages in a particular topic, you can reply to them by going to the bottom of the messages and clicking the Post Reply button.

Neyer's Nuggets

Neyer's Nugget: Search the Newsgroups

I've never entered a chat room in my life because I think the discourse quite often degenerates into either name-calling or messages completely unrelated to the subject at hand. Newsgroups are a cut above chat rooms, but unfortunately I don't participate in them, either. Why? Because for a columnist like me, it's dangerous.

Dangerous? Well, not in the sense that I might suffer bodily harm. But the fact is that so many people now post to newsgroups that practically *everything* has been said by *someone* about practically every subject under the sun. So there's a good chance that anything I write in my column will have been written beforehand by a newsgroup participant. And if I participated in such newsgroups regularly, it wouldn't take a leap of logic for other participants to start thinking that I'm ripping off their ideas. And who knows? I might be doing that, whether purposefully or not. And that's why I don't access newsgroups for baseball information.

I do have a confession to make, however, and I suspect that it will actually be useful to anyone reading this book. There are, of course, many different newsgroups, and if you're looking for news on a particular subject—a specific player, for example—wading through all the relevant newsgroups is a daunting chore. There is an alternative, however. Simply go to Deja.com (*www.deja.com*) and enter your subject in the search box. Lickety-split, you'll be presented with a list of related postings from a variety of different newsgroups. And my confession? From time to time, I'll enter *Rob Neyer* in that search box. Just to see what people are saying about *me*.

Using USENET Newsgroups

When you hear someone referring to "newsgroups," they usually mean USENET Newsgroups. These are a lot like bulletin boards. However, instead of being part of a Web site, they require a separate newsreader program, like Microsoft's Outlook Express.

Newsgroups are a little trickier to use than bulletin boards, too, because you have to "subscribe" to them in order to read the messages in them. I could spend a whole chapter explaining to you how to use USENET Newsgroups using Outlook Express, but that's not really the purpose of this book.

The fact of the matter is that if you can find a link to a specific USENET Newsgroup and click on it, your Outlook Express program will launch, and you'll be reading the newsgroup in no time. So, I've found a shortcut for you—a list of links to USENET Newsgroups.

To see it, go to *www.baseballstuff.com/guide/index.html*. Scroll down the page, and you'll see a list of the newsgroups. There's one for every major league team, and there are many others devoted to baseball as well. In general, the ones that start with "alt" are for fans to post messages about the topic, while the ones that start with "clari" are newsy newsgroups you can read to gather information about your team or topic.

As you can see from the following figure, you'll typically see a list of topics in the upper-right window of Outlook Express, and the messages themselves in the lower-right window.

By the Way:
Since Outlook Express comes as part of Internet Explorer and Windows 98, most people have it installed on their computer, whether they know it or not.

USENET Newsgroups offer fans another outlet for sharing opinions.

Baseball Mailing Lists

Most of us have gotten something strange in the mail at some point and wondered how you ended up on that particular mailing list.

Mailing lists on the Internet aren't quite that way. For example, you can't end up on this type of mailing list accidentally—you have to subscribe to it.

If you're really interested in a particular baseball team or topic, you can find a mailing list for it. Mailing lists are a little like bulletin boards in that when you send a message to the list, everyone else sees it. The key difference is that they have no choice but to see it, because it comes to them as an email.

So, when you're in a mailing list, any message you send to the list will be distributed to every member of the list. Therefore, if you're in a *really* active mailing list, you might end up getting a lot of emails every day. Most mailing lists, however, only generate a few messages a day—sometimes only a couple a week.

> **How Mailing Lists Work:**
>
> Mailing lists are really interesting things. You join a mailing list by sending a subscription message to the "listserv"—the person (or computer) that maintains the list. In most cases, you'll get a confirmation email that welcomes you to the list. Anyone who wants to send a message to the list then addresses it to the listserv. The message goes into the listserv, which then forwards it automatically to every member of the list.

Mailing lists are everywhere. In the last section, you probably came across a couple when you were visiting the Baseball Stuff site for the USENET Newsgroup list.

There's a very complete list of baseball-related mailing lists available at Around the Horn (*www.enteract.com/~bc/bblistservs.html*). You can see a portion of it in the following figure.

You'll note that every mailing list has an "info" address and a "listserv" address. You use the "info" address to subscribe or unsubscribe to a list. Below the two addresses is the message you must put into your email (usually in the message area, not the subject), in order to subscribe. The "listserv" address is the one you use to send a message to the group.

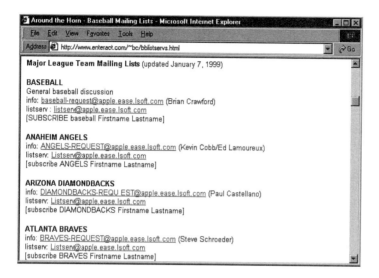

Around the Horn offers a list of mailing lists pertaining to baseball.

Rounding the Bases

Here's a quick look at the stuff we covered in this chapter:

- How chat rooms work, and where you can find them on the Internet.

- The difference between bulletin boards and newsgroups.

- Where you can find bulletin boards and newsgroups for baseball fans.

- How mailing lists work, and where you can find a list of them on the Web.

PART III

Down on the Farm

CHAPTER 8

Minor League Baseball Online

Not every baseball fan is fortunate enough to have a major-league team located in their hometown. In fact, some baseball fans wouldn't even want one.

Minor league baseball has always had a special allure, but the movie *Bull Durham* probably did more for the minor leagues than any other single development in the last 20 years.

Minor league baseball now has its own special following, both in the areas in which it is played and elsewhere in the United States. Some of that might be due to the rising salaries in the majors, as many people believe that the majority of major leaguers have lost touch with the average fan.

The minor leagues, with their low ticket prices and lack of a national television contract, harken back to the old days in the majors. For many fans, it brings back a more innocent time in baseball history.

And heck, it's good baseball. You're guaranteed that the guy playing centerfield isn't coasting through the season, cashing checks, his future secure. Whether the players are veterans working their way back to the Show or youngsters working their way up, chances are pretty good they're giving their best effort.

Every team in the major league has an elaborate minor-league system. These teams, though typically privately owned, have their rosters maintained by the major-league club.

In recent years, a number of "independent" minor leagues have sprung up around the country. These leagues operate independent of Major League Baseball, but some of their players have jumped into traditional minor leagues and even gone to the majors.

What You'll Learn in This Chapter:

▶ How you can follow the minor leagues using typical major-league information providers.

▶ About major services devoted to covering all of minor-league baseball.

▶ How you can follow the farm system of your favorite major-league team.

▶ Where you can find information about a particular minor league and follow it.

▶ Where you can find information about an independent minor league.

▶ How you can follow the Arizona Fall League.

By the Way:

There are a number
of different ways to
go about finding
information on the
minor leagues. We'll
cover most, if not
all, of them in this
chapter.

How you choose to
go about it depends
on your personal
perspective and
wishes—much like
the choice between
reading about the
majors from a big
national service or
your home team's
own Web site.

Another form of minor league, winter ball, has been a staple for players who have needed offseason work to improve. While these leagues have typically been in Latin American countries, the Arizona Fall League has become a developmental league for major-league teams. In this chapter, we'll cover the minors from the fan's perspective.

Information from the Big Boys

One way to learn about, or follow, the minor leagues is to get your information from a big, national provider like ESPN or CBS Sportsline.

Most of the major baseball servers we covered in the previous section of this book offer coverage of the minor leagues in some way, even if it's just standings, stats, and scores.

So if, through the course of reading this book, you've come across a particular service you like for the majors, check to see if they offer any minor-league coverage. If you like the major-league coverage of a particular site, chances are you'll like the minor-league coverage as well.

By the Way:

ESPN's minor league
partner is Baseball
America magazine,
which we'll cover in
the next section of
this chapter.

ESPN's coverage of the minors is typical of what the "big boys" offer. They offer news and feature stories. When it comes to coverage of the leagues themselves, however, it's scores, standings, statistics, schedules, etc.—and even that is only for the higher-level minor leagues.

To make up for that shortcoming, they partner with a provider that offers more detailed coverage of the minor leagues—a very smart move.

For a look at ESPN's main minor-league home page (*http://espn.go.com/minorlbbl*), check out the following figure.

A large service like this is a good place to start if you are not terribly serious about following the minor leagues. It offers the basic information that most fans require.

But if you want to go deeper and get into following teams or leagues, you'll be better off using one of the services in the following section.

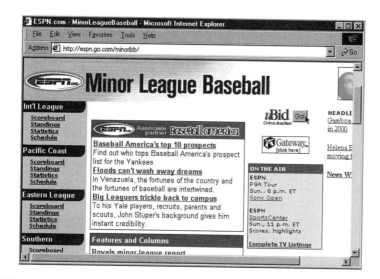

ESPN offers a basic minor-league package that includes standings, schedules, and the like.

Neyer's Nugget: Online Minor League Gurus

A decade or so ago, when I was younger and had more energy, I made great efforts to keep up with the minor leagues. I knew all the top prospects, and I knew the location and affiliation of every minor-league team, thanks to my religious reading of *Baseball America*, a bi-weekly magazine devoted to the minor leagues.

Those days are over. Now I'm in my middle thirties, and I can barely find the time to both follow the major leagues and feed myself. Fortunately, the Web allows me to catch the highlights, so that I can at least give people the *impression* that I know what's going on.

Given that I work for ESPN.com, perhaps I'm a little biased, but I sincerely believe that ESPN.com has the best coverage of the minor leagues you can find. In part, that's due to John Sickels, who in recent years has made a career of tracking and writing about minor leaguers, hundreds of them. During the baseball season, in a feature called "Down on the Farm," Sickels reports on two top prospects every week. Nowhere else on the Web or in print will you find such detailed, timely, and objective evaluations. Sickels's reports have a different Web address every week, but you can find them in the "Features and Columns" section of ESPN.com's main baseball page.

continues

continued

In addition to Sickels, ESPN.com is fortunate to have the aforementioned *Baseball America* as an "Associate partner." What does this mean? It means that you don't have to memorize or bookmark *Baseball America*'s Web address. Simply find ESPN.com's baseball page, scroll to the bottom, and you'll find links to a few current *Baseball America* stories, plus a link to the *Baseball America* site itself. And in one of these two places, you'll likely find the work of David Rawnsley, who ranks with Sickels as one of the country's top experts on minor-league prospects. Rawnsley, who once worked for the Houston Astros, is perhaps the only national analyst with both a traditional scouting background and a solid knowledge of statistical analysis. That combination makes him among the very best at what he does.

Large Services Devoted to the Minor Leagues

Sometimes, the big boys don't have everything it takes. Here's a good example of why you might want to check out one of the sites in this section: If you're looking for a lot of information about hammers, you'll generally get better results going to a hardware store than you will going to a hardware department in a large discount retailer.

Consider the sites we cover in this section to be hardware stores. They concentrate on coverage of the minor leagues, and thus do a better job of it.

Baseball America Online

Baseball America is a national magazine devoted to covering baseball, especially at the minor-league level. The printed magazine is a great source for baseball information, and Baseball America Online is, too.

The online version does a great job of putting perspective on the minor leagues. It offers Top 10 prospect lists in a variety of different ways. For example, you can get a list of the Top 10 prospects in the Midwest League, or you can get the list of Top 10 prospects in the Arizona Diamondbacks organization.

The site can be found at *www.baseballamerica.com*. You can see it in the following figure.

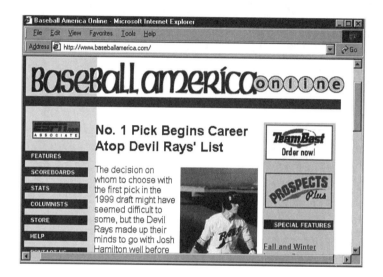

Baseball America's online version keeps you up-to-date about the minors.

The site offers scoreboards, stats, and standings from around minor-league baseball, but goes beyond that to offer feature stories and even columnists. And, just like the printed magazine, Baseball America Online also covers college and high school baseball.

In addition, they cover the winter leagues, and offer complete lists of minor-league transactions. It's a great resource for following that local kid who signed with a major-league organization.

By the Way:
We'll cover college and high school baseball in the next two chapters. Chapter 9 is entitled, "College Baseball Online," and Chapter 10 is called, "Amateur Baseball Online."

The National Association of Professional Baseball Leagues

The National Association of Professional Baseball Leagues oversees all of minor-league baseball (except the independent leagues, of course). It also maintains what it calls "the official site of Minor League Baseball" at *www.minorleaguebaseball.com*.

You can see it in the following figure.

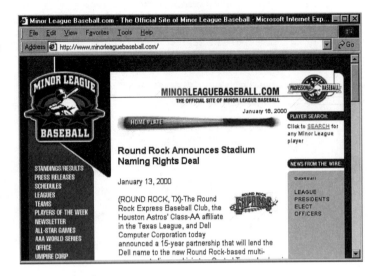

Again, you can use this site to find schedules, standings and
results during the minor league seasons. But because this is the
governing body of the minor leagues, this site's true value comes
in its archives of general minor-league information.

For example, right on the main page you'll see a list of league
champions for the previous season. There are also pages devoted
to specific leagues and specific teams.

But one of the things that can get confusing about minor-league
baseball is just which team belongs to which major-league organization. This site helps sort all that out. Let's take a walk through it.

Try It Yourself ▼

1. Go to the Minor League Baseball site at
   www.minorleaguebaseball.com.

2. Click on the button on the left side called Teams.

3. If you know the name of the team, you can find it in the
   alphabetical listing of teams, click on its name and you'll find
   out which organization it belongs to.

4. If you want the complete list of teams that belong to a particular major-league organization, click on Major League
   Affiliation Listing.

5. Find the organization you're interested in, and you'll see the complete list of minor-league teams that belong to it.

Finding Affiliates of Major-League Teams:

Another way to locate the minor-league affiliates of a major-league team is to go to the major-league team's Web site.

That's often the best way, because you'll get more detailed information about the minor-league affiliates, including links to their Web site, if they have one.

Back in Chapter 5, we offered a complete list of Web sites for every team in the majors. Go to your team's Web site, and you'll probably see a "Minor League" or "Down on the Farm" button or link you can click to find the information you seek.

Following a Particular League

If you live in an area that is served by a particular minor league, you might want to follow that entire league online, just as major-league fans follow the entire American or National League (or all of Major League Baseball, for that matter).

There are a couple of ways to do that. First, you can use one of the sites already covered in this chapter to get the basic information on scores, standings, and so on.

However, if you want to go beyond the basics and get into more detail about a specific league, try to locate that league's Web site. Not a lot of individual leagues have them, unfortunately (although a lot of individual *teams* have sites).

One league that does have a site is the Class AAA International League (*www.ilbaseball.com*). You can see it in the following figure.

As baseball has become big business, there has been a lot of franchise movement, especially in the lower levels of minor league baseball. The International League, however, is made up of some of the oldest minor-league franchises around, such as the Pawtucket Red Sox, Durham Bulls, Toledo Mud Hens, Columbus Clippers, and Buffalo Bisons.

The International League's Web site is a complete resource for fans of the league. Everything from links to the Web sites of each of the individual teams to Players of the Week to Names in the News, you'll find what you're looking for here.

One Man's Opinion:

If you are going to use one of the sites that covers the minors in general to follow a specific league, I recommend *www.minorleague-baseball.com* for general information about each of the minor leagues. For scores, standings, and so on, I recommend one of the "big boys" like ESPN or CBS Sportsline.

*The International
League's Web site
does a great job
of following the
league.*

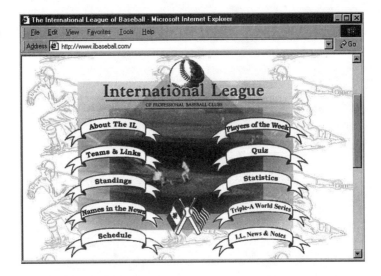

Independent Minor Leagues

Over the past few years, independent minor leagues have sprung up around the country. In the beginning, they were controversial, in that the major-league organizations were not fond of having to compete for players at the lowest levels.

One of the first was the Northern League, which was initially based in the Upper Midwest.

The Northern League has grown from six teams in Minnesota, the Dakotas, Iowa, and Canada to a 16-team league with two divisions and franchises stretching from the Dakotas to the Eastern seaboard.

Renegade, Maverick, or Merely Good Businessman?

Mike Veeck, son of the late baseball pioneer Bill Veeck, was one of the initial owners of the St. Paul Saints, the cornerstone franchise of the Northern League. He helped bring legitimacy to the league by bringing in big-name ex-major leaguers who were trying to make their way back.

Veeck emphasized atmosphere, outdoor baseball (in competition with the Twins in the Metrodome), and had plenty of sideshows going on between innings to keep fans having fun.

It worked.

The league has not been in existence for long, but one of the Saints who's made a name for himself is Rey Ordonez, now shortstop for the New York Mets.

Among others who have played for the Saints are Darryl Strawberry (on his way back from rehabilitation), Jack Morris (on his way out of baseball), and J.D. Drew (while he waited for a major-league contract that was to his liking).

You can visit the Web site at *www.northernleague.com*, and you can see it in the following figure.

The Northern League has grown to 16 teams from the original six.

This site, like the International League's site, is a very complete resource for fans. In a league that changes as rapidly as the Northern League has, you need to be able to communicate with fans. The Northern League Web site accomplishes this by offering a Press Releases area so you can keep up with new franchises and stadiums around the league.

Arizona Fall League

The Arizona Fall League was set up by the major leagues in order to offer players a greater chance to develop in the offseason while maintaining contact with their major-league organizations.

Previously, players had to go to Latin American countries in order to get that experience, and many in the majors felt they weren't getting the type of instruction they needed.

There are six franchises in the Arizona Fall League. Each franchise is made up of players from five different major-league organizations. For example, the Mesa Solar Sox includes players from the White Sox, Red Sox, Cubs, Pirates, and Rangers organizations.

Here are a couple of options for fans interested in following their prospects in the Arizona Fall League:

- **Major League Baseball's site** (*www.majorleaguebaseball.com/ u/baseball/mlbcom/1999/afl/*)   Since the AFL is an offshoot of Major League Baseball, this is a good site for fans. It offers coverage of the games and more, including feature stories on individual players. During the 1999 AFL season, one player wrote a diary for use on the Web page.

- **Squeezebunt.com's site** (*www.squeezebunt.com/azfall.html*) Squeezebunt.com covers baseball in Arizona, including the fall league and Major League Baseball's spring training Cactus League. The site includes everything from team information to a driving guide that offers distance between the stadiums.

Rounding the Bases

In this chapter, we took a look at baseball's minor leagues and what's available for fans on the Web. We covered:

- Minor-league resources available from the "big boys" like ESPN.

- Major Web servers devoted primarily to coverage of Minor League Baseball.

- How to find information about the league you are most interested in.

- Where you can find information on the farm system of a particular major-league organization.

- Independent minor leagues and what they offer on the Web.

- Where you can find information about the Arizona Fall League.

CHAPTER 9

College Baseball Online

For pure, raw baseball excitement, it's hard to beat the College World Series. Some baseball purists don't like it because the aluminum bats produce too much scoring, but when it comes to players giving their all and games going down to the wire, the College World Series has got it.

Time was when college baseball was an afterthought for most up-and-coming baseball stars. Most of them looked for that big-league contract and a chance to work their way up through the minor leagues.

Over the years, however, more and more players came through the college ranks to professional stardom. Roger Clemens and Mark McGwire, just to name a couple, exemplify the type of player that the college ranks can produce.

In recent years, more and more major-league teams are looking to the colleges in the early rounds of the draft, because they find they are getting a more polished product.

Aside from all that, college baseball is just plain fun. Those of us in the northern half of the United States probably don't have the same appreciation for it that southern residents have. But college baseball is growing in popularity all over the country.

Just as the popularity of the sport itself has grown, so has its popularity on the Web. These days, you can find information about college baseball all over the Internet.

There are several major services that cover college baseball from top to bottom. Many conferences across the country—at all levels—maintain Web sites. In addition, many individual universities maintain Web sites for the teams that represent them. In this chapter, we'll cover all of that.

What You'll Learn in This Chapter:

▶ Where to find the latest information about college baseball—the scores, standings and so on.

▶ How conferences around the country provide information for the college baseball fan.

▶ Individual college teams' Web sites, and where to find them.

▶ Where to find information on the College World Series, including how to follow it live online.

By the Way:

Up here in Minnesota, we may not have had success at a national level like many southern schools have, but the University of Minnesota's baseball program has produced Dave Winfield, Paul Molitor, Terry Steinbach, and Denny Neagle, just to name a few.

Keeping Up with the Latest

Regardless of the level of baseball you like to follow, you need a source to help you keep up with the latest news, scores and so on.

College baseball is no different. The season gets rolling when spring is still a glimmer in most people's eyes, and you're going to need a source to help you keep track of it all.

There are lots of great sources out there on the Web for college baseball fans. As usual, you can try to get your information from a big sports service, which might offer a college baseball page. Some even offer pretty good coverage of the sport.

But let's take a look at some sites that are devoted solely to the college baseball fan.

College Sports News Baseball Page

The College Sports News offers coverage of all major college sports throughout the year. It does a good job of covering baseball as well.

You can check out the CollegeSports News baseball site at *http://chili.collegesportsnews.com/baseball/default.htm.* You can see it in the following figure.

College Sports News' Baseball page offers the latest baseball news.

In the upper-left corner of the figure, you can see that baseball scores, stats, and standings are available for fans to use.

The site also offers a Newsroom and feature stories, plus links to a number of different polls for ranking college teams.

It's a good place for the college baseball fan to start.

FANSonly

A site named "FANSonly" should be a top-notch site for fans, and this one doesn't fall short.

Like College Sports News, FANSonly covers a variety of collegiate sports. Its baseball coverage can be found at *www.FANSonly.com/ channels/news/sports/m-basebl/*. You can see it in the following figure.

By the Way:

We'll cover sites for individual teams later in this chapter.

FANSonly offers breaking news about college baseball.

Like the big professional sports services, FANSonly maintains team pages for individual schools around the country.

It highlights top news stories as they happen, keeping fans up-to-date on the latest in college baseball. Just recently, however, the site added bulletin boards so that fans can post messages to each other and read the opinions of others.

If you really want to get into the nitty-gritty of college baseball, check out the recruiting link for the latest on which high school players are signing where.

By the Way:

If you need more information about bulletin boards and how they work, read Chapter 7, "Talkin' Baseball—The Hot Stove League."

Collegiate Baseball Stats

If it's statistics that you are looking for, the NCAA has the solution for you. Just visit their stats site at *www.ncaa.org/ stats/baseball.cgi*.

You'll find a series of drop-down menus that you can use to pull up the latest statistics. Some of the stats aren't updated until the end of the season, but the basic stuff like batting averages are kept up-to-date throughout the season.

You can even have the stats emailed to you if that's what you'd like.

Following Your Conference

Before teams can get to the College World Series, they have to fight their way through their conference schedule. In many conferences, there is also a conference tournament at the end of the season.

Conference games go a long way toward determining who will get berths in the NCAA Regionals that lead up to the College World Series. And, as in other sports, conference matchups also generate great rivalries over the years.

If you live in an area in which college baseball is a big-time sport, then you probably have a conference that you tend to follow more than the others. The chances are good that that conference has its own Web site.

Many conference Web sites—most, in fact—are devoted to all sports, not just baseball. But they usually have a button or link on the main page that takes you directly to the baseball portion of the site.

The Big 12 Conference

The Big 12 Conference includes some of the best college baseball programs in the country. Perennial powers like Texas A&M, Baylor, Texas Tech, Oklahoma State, Texas, and more battle it out every year for supremacy in what is one of the toughest baseball conferences in the land.

To get to the Big 12's baseball Web site, you can go to the main Big 12 page at *www.big12sports.com* and click the baseball button. Or, you can go directly to the baseball pages at *www.big12sports.com/bbo/bbc/index.html*. The baseball home page is seen in the following figure.

The Big 12 features some of the top teams in the country.

During the season, you can follow Big 12 baseball in detail, with stats, standings, game recaps and summaries, and so on. You can even take a look back at seasons past.

This site is also comprehensive enough to offer some extra historical features that make for interesting reading. For example, you can find a list of Big 12 alumni who have played in the Major League Baseball World Series over the years—in 1999, it was Roger Clemens (Texas) and Chuck Knoblauch (Texas A&M).

Some Big 12 games are even TotalCast during the season, just as many major league games are. For those games, you can get pitch-by-pitch accounts of every at-bat, including a diagram of pitch locations.

SEC Baseball Web Site

The Southeastern Conference, or SEC, is another of the top conferences in the country. It features a number of strong teams every year, including powers Louisiana State, Alabama, and Arkansas.

The SEC Baseball Web site is a strong one that offers many of the same features as the Big 12's site. It can be found at *www.sec.org/teams/base/* and can be seen in the following figure.

In addition to regular coverage of the season, the site offers a conference record book and a record book for each individual team in the league.

Since this conference is located in a college baseball hotbed, many of the games are carried on regional sports cable networks. The conference's entire television schedule is available on the Web site, so you can follow the action.

The SEC Web site highlights some of the top teams in the country.

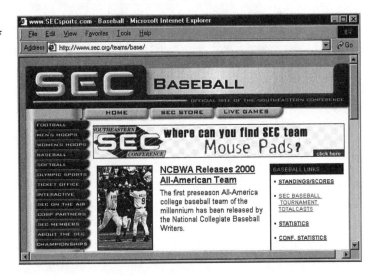

Individual Team Sites

Dozens of college baseball teams have sites on the Internet that are devoted to them. There are a couple of different ways to find them.

If you know the Web address of the university whose team you would like to follow, you can go to that site and probably navigate your way to the baseball team's page(s). If the conference has a site, you can often get to individual teams' sites from there as well.

Miami (Florida) University is typically one of the top teams in the country. The Hurricanes won the College World Series in 1999.

Let's find our way to the Hurricanes baseball team's site.

1. Go to the Miami Hurricanes main sports Web page at *www.hurricanesports.com.*

2. In the drop-down menu on the home page, where it says Choose Sport, select Baseball.

3. You will automatically go to Miami's baseball page at FANSonly. You're there!

▼ **Try It Yourself**

▲

Why Is It a FANSonly Page?

FANSonly is an organization that offers online management to collegiate athletic departments. So many schools have opted to have FANSonly manage their Web site.

Unlike a provider like ESPN, however, where the pages for all the major-league teams are virtually identical, FANSonly college team pages are unique. So the Miami Hurricanes' pages are different than those of other teams who use the FANSonly service.

You can see the Hurricanes Web page in the following figure.

Miami's Web page highlights its 1999 national championship.

Not all universities use FANSonly to handle their Internet needs. The University of Michigan, for example, does not. You can see the Wolverines' Web site at *http://mgoblue.com/baseball/*. Check it out in the following figure.

The University of Michigan's baseball team has its own Web site.

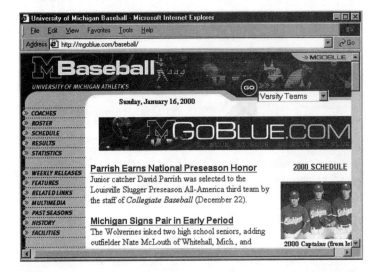

The College World Series

All Division 1 college teams start out with one dream—to reach the College World Series. The most elite among them have an even loftier dream, to win it.

Every year, Rosenblatt Stadium in Omaha, Nebraska becomes the focal point of the baseball world for a brief period of time. The top eight college teams in the nation reach the College World Series after qualifying in regionals around the country.

Once they are there, they play off in a double-elimination format that is one of the best showcases of college athletics in any sport.

During this time period (and throughout the year, really), the official College World Series Web site chronicles every move.

The site is located at *www.ncaabaseball.com*, and can be seen in the following figure.

The official Web site of the College World Series keeps fans abreast of the tournament's events.

All of the games in the tournament are available as TotalCast, so you can follow them pitch-by-pitch.

There's a live scoreboard running on the page at all times, and you can view the entire tournament bracket to stay aware of which teams have suffered a loss and must win the rest of their games or be eliminated. You can also use it to forecast upcoming matchups.

There's a great CWS history page as well, to shed some light on the teams and players that have made the event so great over the years.

What About the Other Levels?

Not everything happens at the Division 1 level, of course. There's great baseball being played at all levels of collegiate sports.

If you're looking for a site that covers national championships at all levels, check out *www.ncaachampionships.com/sports/base/*.

It covers everything from tournament brackets to television schedules to team mascots for the national championships at all levels.

Rounding the Bases

This was a chapter for the college baseball fan, particularly those who follow Division 1 collegiate baseball.

Here's what we covered:

- How to keep up with the latest college baseball news, scores, stats and standings using big servers devoted to the sport.

- How major conferences use the Internet to support their leagues and what fans of particular conferences can find on the Web.

- What you can find for sites of individual college baseball teams on the Web.

- Where to look for information about the College World Series.

CHAPTER 10

Amateur Baseball Online

Depending on your perspective, you could say that the last seven chapters of this book have been written backwards.

Go back to chapter 4, and you'll see that we started with Major League Baseball. After a few chapters of that, we moved on to the minor leagues, then to college, and now to amateur baseball.

Well, anyone who's made it to the big leagues has started playing somewhere along the line. Whether that was tee-ball, Little League or, in the most rare of cases, high school, they all got their start in their youth.

(Even Michael Jordan, while he didn't embark on a professional career until he was an adult, played baseball as a youth.)

That's what this chapter is all about.

For every level of amateur baseball, there are tons of organizations that serve it. There are associations and congresses and unions and leagues and organizations all over this country. A lot of them have Web sites for their member teams, coaches, and players.

We're not going to cover all the regional and local organizations that govern baseball at various levels in detail—there's just too many of them. We will give you some examples of larger organizations and what they offer their members.

Heck, since the book's been backwards from the get go, we might as well write this chapter backwards, too. So we'll start with American Legion, Babe Ruth, and high school baseball, where the older kids play.

We'll move back to youth and PONY league baseball before heading even further down the chain to Little League Baseball.

What You'll Learn in This Chapter:

▶ American Legion baseball, including the national organization and an example of information from an individual league.

▶ Other high-school age baseball, including Babe Ruth, AAU, and high school ball itself.

▶ How you can find a tournament in which your local team can compete.

▶ Resources for youth and amateur baseball at all levels.

▶ Youth baseball, including PONY and Little League and the Little League World Series.

By the Way:

This chapter will not only serve the fans of amateur baseball, but it will also provide information for coaches, players, and league organizers who participate in amateur baseball.

American Legion, Babe Ruth, and High School Baseball

About a million kids play, either American Legion or Babe Ruth Baseball at one of many levels they offer. These are two of a number of different organizing bodies that set rules and guidelines for their associations.

On the local level, teams compete representing their city, regional area or, in the case of Legion, an American Legion Post. Local leagues are organized regionally, and champions can advance to state, region and, in some cases, national championship tournaments.

These national organizing bodies have set up Web sites to offer information to both people already involved and those who are considering getting involved.

American Legion's Web Site

Almost 100,000 players age 15-18 played American Legion baseball in 1999, according to the Legion's own Web site at *www.legion.org/baseball/home.htm*.

High school-age kids may play for their schools during the spring and convert to a Legion team for the summer months. It gives them another outlet to play more games against good competition, which helps them improve, of course.

The Legion's Web site offers a great deal of information for people who are interested in Legion ball, and it offers it from a number of different perspectives. You can see the site in the following figure.

Let's take a look at the site from these perspectives:

- **For the organizer:** If you're interested in forming an American Legion team, you must work with a local American Legion Post. The link on the Web site called Finding or Forming a Legion Team will help you, as will the link to State Baseball Chairmen Directory.

- **For the coach:** The above links will help you if you're trying to track down other Legion teams to play against. There's also a link for Legion baseball rules and another that leads to copies of forms that players must fill out.

- **For the fan:** The History and Facts links are interesting, but there's more. The Graduates of the Year link leads to the list of major-leaguers who have been honored by the Legion for their play and commitment to community. There's also links for regional champions and state titleholders.

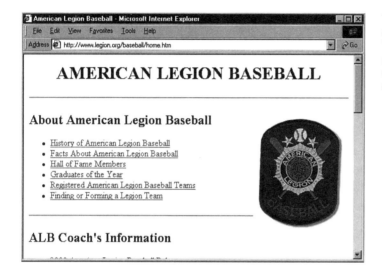

The American Legion's baseball Web site has information for organizers, coaches, and fans.

Babe Ruth League, Inc.'s Web Site

Babe Ruth Baseball is also played at the high school level across the country, and it offers a division for 13–15 year olds as well.

Babe Ruth League, Inc. was formed in the 1950s in Trenton, New Jersey, and quickly grew to be a national organization. Last year, almost 900,000 kids played Babe Ruth baseball at one of its two levels.

Over the years, Babe Ruth has grown and now offers three levels of girls' softball: 12 and under, 16 and under, and 18 and under. The latest edition to the lineup is baseball for ages 5-12, which they are calling Cal Ripken Baseball.

Babe Ruth League's Web site (*www.baberuthleague.org*) has a ton of resources. You can see it in the following figure.

In addition to historical information, you can learn about the different divisions and league information. There's even information about baseball camps for players to attend.

Babe Ruth League, Inc.'s Web site includes a wealth of information.

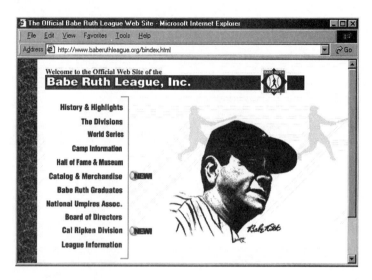

One Man's Opinion:

I spent two years coaching 16-year-olds in American Legion baseball and also some time working for a college recruiting service. If you or someone you know wants to be considered as a college athlete in any sport, take this advice: Keep the grades up. There are thousands of young people competing for not very many scholarships. And while you hear a lot about "borderline" students who get college scholarships, that's the exception, not the rule. Given a choice between two players of equal talent, the college coach is going to take the good student every time.

The World Series link leads to information about dates and location of the upcoming Babe Ruth World Series (at all levels), but also offers results of some previous World Series.

Local League's Web Site

Many local leagues in both American Legion and Babe Ruth baseball have set up Web sites to make it easier for fans, coaches and players alike to keep up with the latest.

A good example of such as site is the Lower Montco (Pennsylvania) League of American Legion baseball. It is located at *http://lmontco.freeservers.com*, and you can see it in the following figure.

There's a great page that offers information for prospective players, and there's a page for every team in the league. There's even a page for college coaches to go to that lists the name and statistical information of league players who have an interest in playing baseball in college. There's also a page for such players to read that includes information on how to become a college baseball player.

There are also, of course, links to standings and other league information for those who are currently playing. There's also an Alumni News page that keeps you up-to-date with the latest on former league players.

Lower Montco American Legion's site provides information for current and prospective players.

High School Baseball

High schools across the nation offer baseball programs, generally in the spring (after all, that's when a young man's fancy turns to thoughts of baseball, right?).

There are lots of Internet resources for those interested in high school baseball. You can check with your state's governing body of high school sports to see if they have a Web site, or look for a site for your school's conference.

One great national resource is the High School Baseball Web (*www.hsbaseballweb.com*). You can see it in the following figure.

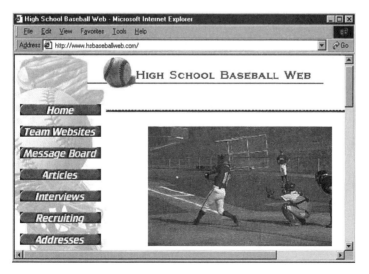

The High School Baseball Web is for anyone interested in high school baseball.

One Man's Opinion:

If you want a good example of a high school baseball team's Web site, scroll down to Minnesota and click in the link to The Blake School. It's very thorough and informative for a high school team's site.

It's an informative site for kids (and their parents) who want to play in college or professionally. One of the best aspects of this site is the Message Board, which appears to be very active with hundreds of posts. There's some great idea-exchanging going on there.

In addition, the Team Websites link takes you to a state-by-state list of high school teams that have their own sites on the Internet.

Baseball for the Littler People

You don't have to be a high-schooler to play baseball, of course. It all starts back in Little League and leads up through the lower teens.

Little League Baseball and other organizations such as PONY League offer younger kids a great opportunity to build a level of enjoyment of the game. For those who are already tough competitors, there are national competitions for kids at these levels, too. And with Little League, of course, there's a *real* World Series in which they face off against international competition.

PONY League Baseball

PONY (Protect Our Nation's Youth) started with kids age 13-15, but now offers programs to both boys and girls (softball) ages 5-18. More than a half-million kids are now part of the program.

PONY's Web site at *www.pony.org* offers teams a chance to register to join the organization and, of course, includes information about rules, tournaments, and so on.

It's a good resource for players and others interested in the PONY organization.

Little League Baseball

It's all fun and games at the Little League level, right? Depending on your perspective, not necessarily.

Whether you've been able to keep your focus or you're sure your little guy is headed for the big leagues, Little League baseball is genuine fun. (Or, at least it *should* be.)

Most kids who toil on the local diamonds scooping up grounders while picking dandelions never make it to the big-time stage that is the Little League World Series. But that's the Holy Grail for 12-year-olds, and it's held in Williamsport, Pennsylvania, every year.

Little League Baseball, however, isn't just for 12-year-olds. It starts much younger, and its four divisions extend all the way through high school age.

Little League has a Web site at *www.littleleague.org*. You can see it in the following figure.

Little League offers baseball at all levels.

Each level of Little League baseball culminates its play every year with a World Series that brings together players from around the globe.

Let's take a walk through the site to information about the most famous of the World Series, the 12-year-old version.

▼ **Try It Yourself**

1. Go to the Little League Web site at www.littleleague.org.

2. Click on the World Series button on the left side of the page. Then click on the World Series logo on the next page.

3. Click Little League Baseball from either the logo in the middle of the page or the menu on the left.

▲

Once you're at the World Series page, you can get profiles of the teams, a multimedia virtual tour, and much, much more. This is a very interactive and extensive site, especially during the actual playing of the World Series itself.

Other Amateur Baseball Resources

As you go down the levels of baseball, you'll find less and less information on the Web. So amateur baseball doesn't have the extensive list of sites that the major leagues do, and it probably never will.

But the number and quality of Web resources for amateur baseball aficionados grows every day. Let's take a look at a couple of other resources for the amateur baseball fan or player.

AAU Baseball

The Amateur Athletic Union sponsors national competitions in a wide variety of sports including baseball. AAU teams can be local teams that are part of another organization, such as Legion or Babe Ruth teams. They can also be separate teams that are put together on a regional level to compete in AAU events.

AAU offers a Web site specifically for baseball at *www.aaubaseball.org*. You can see it in the following figure.

AAU Baseball offers national tournaments at a high level of competition.

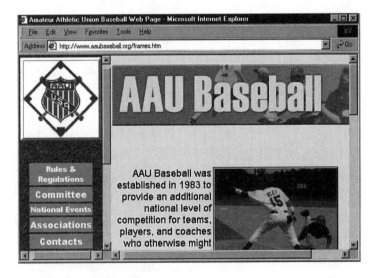

A quick tour of this site will help you determine if your team or player will want to compete at this level. One link takes you to a Rules and Regulations page that will help you prepare your team for AAU competition.

Competitive Baseball Web

One of the best aspects of youth sports is playing in a tournament against teams you don't normally play. Every traveling team I've ever coached, I made sure to get into a tournament, preferably out of town so we could play new teams. And, taking a "road trip" was always fun, too.

The Competitive Baseball Web (*www.cbweb.com*) acts as a kind of tournament clearing house for teams at all levels. There's a database of active tournaments from all over the country, and there's a News page that acts as a message board for teams.

On the News page, you'll find notes from coaches all over the country who are looking for games for their teams. It's a great way to fill out a schedule.

Rounding the Bases

Amateur baseball resources on the Web are growing every day. Here is a list of things we covered in this chapter:

- Where to find information for high-school age players, including American Legion, Babe Ruth, and high school baseball Web sites.

- How individual leagues and teams use the Internet to provide information to players and fans.

- Where to find information about Little League and other organizations for younger players.

- Other national resources for amateur baseball, including AAU tournament and other tournament information.

CHAPTER 11

International Baseball Online

What You'll Learn in This Chapter:

▶ Where to find information about Japanese professional baseball, the league and the individual teams.

▶ Where to find information about baseball in other countries.

▶ How to use the Internet for information about baseball in the Olympics and other international baseball competitions.

Most fans of Major League Baseball, I'd guess, have heard of Hideki Irabu and Hideo Nomo.

Nomo was the Japanese sensation who came to America with the Los Angeles Dodgers and took the National League by storm. Irabu was the much-publicized fireballer, also from Japan, who eventually signed with the Yankees.

More and more Japanese baseball players have come to the U.S. to play in the major leagues in recent years. But long before Nomo, baseball has had more of an international flair than any other major professional sports league.

For years, major-league organizations have left the U.S. to find talent, particularly in Latin American countries. The list of Latin-born players is too long to recount, but it includes the likes of Juan Marichal, Roberto Clemente, the Alou brothers, the Alomar brothers (and their dad, Sandy Sr.), Ivan Rodriguez, and on and on.

Even some players from Cuba, most notably Livan and Orlando Hernandez in recent years, have made impacts at the major-league level.

The point here is this: Baseball is played all over the world. And while some of that baseball ends up impacting baseball in America, the vast majority of it doesn't. Other countries have their own leagues, their own stars.

This chapter will look at baseball in other countries and international baseball competitions, such as the Olympic Games.

One Man's Opinion:

If you're thinking that a player arriving from Cuba is only a recent phenomenon, think again. While the Hernandezes have been well-publicized defectors, there was a period in history when diplomatic relations with Cuba were less strained so that several Cuban players made it to America to play. One of those players was a favorite from my youth—Tony Oliva.

The Challenge of International Baseball:

Like the players and coaches have in many international competitions, we encountered somewhat of a language barrier in researching this chapter.

Part of the difficulty in using the Internet to find information about international baseball is that the Internet is a worldwide phenomenon. As such, when you come across a Japanese baseball site, for example, it is often set up for Japanese users—written in Japanese.

Many sites will offer an English-language mirror site, but some don't. For purposes of this book, which will have a largely English-speaking audience, we have concentrated on English-language sites.

Japanese Baseball

Here's a quick quiz for all you baseball trivia experts: Who holds the record for the most home runs in professional baseball?

The quick answer might be Hank Aaron, with 755. But if you include Japan's highest level of baseball in the equation, the answer would be Sadaharu Oh, who hit 868 home runs from 1959 to 1980 for the Tokyo Giants.

Oh is just one of many Japanese baseball heroes whose names have become familiar to baseball fans here in America. But it's gone the other way, too. Many American baseball players have gone overseas and had successful careers in Japanese baseball. Some have even become heroes in their own right in Japan.

Neyer's Nuggets

Neyer's Nugget: Japanese Pitchers and Other Players

Until relatively recently, the extent of most American baseball fans' knowledge of Japanese baseball began and ended with Sadaharu Oh. A few "experts" also knew about American players who thrived in Japan—players like Randy Bass and Warren Cromartie—but for the most part, the two games were separated by both the Pacific Ocean and a gulf of knowledge.

All that has changed in recent years. Until 1995, only one Japanese-born player had ever served with a Major League Baseball team. (That one player was Masanori Murakami, who pitched 54 games for the San Francisco Giants in 1964 and 1965.) But in 1995, pitcher Hideo Nomo made a huge splash with the Los Angeles Dodgers. Since then, a number of other Japanese-born pitchers have appeared in the major leagues, including Hideki Irabu, Mac Suzuki, Masato Yoshii, and Shigetoshi Hasegawa. As a result, fans have been scurrying to Web sites that list stats for all these heretofore-unknown hurlers.

Given the recent influx of Japanese pitchers, some fundamental questions naturally arise: Where are the Japanese *non*pitchers? There must be some Japanese outfielders—to name just one position—capable of playing at the highest level of professional baseball, right?

The answer to the latter query is, *of course there are*. So why haven't we seen any Japanese nonpitchers? Well, it's a two-fold answer. First of all, there might be some cultural bias going on here. Japanese hitters tend to be smaller than their American counterparts, and many American scouts typically have little interest in short ballplayers (unless they play great defense at shortstop). Second, the game in Japan makes it easier to spot the great pitchers. The ballparks there generally favor the hitters, so if you see a Japanese pitcher with outstanding statistics, you know he's probably an outstanding pitcher. Eventually, we'll see Japanese hitters in *our* major leagues. But they've got a lot of catching up to do.

Whether you're looking for information about an American-born player in Japan or just interested in following Japanese professional baseball, you can do at the league's official Web site at *www.inter.co.jp/baseball/*. You can see the site in the following figure.

This address leads to an English-language portion of this site, allowing you a glimpse of Japan's highest level of baseball competition.

You can dig around this site without running into a language barrier, but a certain click here or there can end up in a roadblock.

If it's information on non-Japanese players you're looking for, this site makes it easy for you. Just click on the link to any given season, and it opens a page of statistics. At the top of the page, however, you'll get links to "Players from Outside Japan," giving you access to their stats separately.

By the Way:
It's here, for example, that you can learn that former major-leaguer Willie Banks was 3-3 with a 3.94 earned run average for the Orix Blue Wave in 1999.

Japanese professional baseball offers an English-language site.

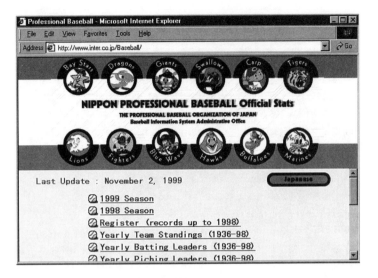

There's a lot more information here if you just scroll down the page. You can find complete statistics for the current and past seasons, and you can get linescores and stats from any given day during the season using the menu on the left.

Back on the main page, however, you'll see a little button that says "Japanese" on the right side of the screen (refer back to the previous figure). That's an inkling of what's to come if you delve too deeply into this site.

If you try to find information about one of the teams using their logo from the top of the page, you actually switch to the Japanese version of the site.

Try It Yourself ▼

Just for fun, let's try to learn a little more about the Fukuoka Daiei Hawks.

1. From the main Japanese professional baseball home page (*www.inter.co.jp/baseball/*), click on the Hawks logo near the top of the screen.

2. You are moved to the Hawks' home page at *www.hawkstown.com*, as you can see in the following figure. There are some English words, but most of the site is in Japanese.

3. Toward the upper-left of the page, there is a button called English. Click it.

▲   4. You are switched to the English-language version of the site.

Hawks Town is the
official home
page of the
Fukuoka Daiei
Hawks.

By the Way:
Not all of the 12
Japanese league
teams offer English
versions of their
sites.

The English-language site doesn't appear to have as much to offer,
but you can read about the Fukuoka Dome, the first retractable-
roof stadium in Japan, and other interesting notes. If you want
more information about the team itself, you're better off staying on
the league's main page.

Baseball in the Olympics

Baseball made its debut as a medal sport in the Olympics at the
Barcelona Games in 1992. Cuba, not surprisingly, has won the
gold medal both times, heading into the 2000 Games in Sydney,
Australia.

Baseball had been a demonstration sport in the Olympics on
many different occasions, most notably in 1984, when a group of
collegiate stars led by Mark McGwire highlighted the Games in
Los Angeles.

Since 2000 is an Olympic year, there will be more and more
available on the Web as the games grow nearer. There are a couple of sites you might want to visit if you are fan of baseball in
the Olympics.

NBC's Olympics Site

NBC paid about a kazillion dollars for the rights to broadcast the
Olympics until the year 4545. Something like that. As a result,
they are making sure that their coverage is thorough, both on television and on the Web.

Mission accomplished.

Even eight months before the Games, NBC's Olympics site (*www.nbcolympics.com*) is jam-packed with information. One can only imagine what it will be like during the Games themselves.

NBC's Olympics site has information about every sport, including baseball.

To help you get ready, go to their site and select Baseball from the drop-down menu called Choose a Sport. The result will be similar to what you see in the following figure.

Here you can get the latest news on the U.S. team and other teams from around the world, including coverage of pre-Olympic events featuring the teams that will meet in Sydney.

Official Olympics Site

By the Way:

Since the major-league season is still going on during the Olympics, the U.S. will send a team of minor-league players to the Games in Sydney.

The 2000 Games in Sydney is the first time professional baseball players will be allowed to compete in the Olympics. Even though the United States won't be sending a Dream Team of major leaguers, the ruling could challenge Cuba's reign as two-time defending gold medalists, according to the official Olympics Web site.

To go straight to the baseball page, use the following address: *www.olympics.com/eng/sports/BB/about/*. You can see it in the following figure.

You can learn about the official Olympic rules for baseball, find out when and where the games will be played (including the qualifying tournaments), and much more.

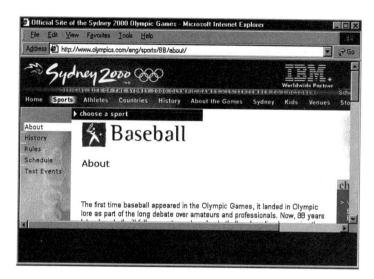

The official Olympic site offers a baseball page as well.

By the way:

If you are a fan of the Olympics in general, go to *www.olympics.com/ eng/*. That's the English-language home page for the entire Olympic Games.

At this writing, this page includes an interesting history of baseball in the Games that is worth reading for any baseball fan. It covers baseball's involvement in the debate over amateurs vs. professionals in the Games.

Other International Baseball Resources

Let's take a quick walk through some of the better international resources for baseball fans.

International Baseball Association

The International Baseball Association sponsors international competitions such as the World Cup and Intercontinental Cup.

The IBA's Web site at *www.baseball.ch* is a good resource for people who want to keep tabs on these events.

You can learn about the organization, its rules, and its competitions here.

USA Baseball's Site

USA Baseball is the organization that governs national teams at levels ranging from 16-and-under to the Olympic teams.

The USA Baseball Web site (*www.usabaseball.com*) includes information on all of these teams. Their schedules, rosters, results and more are available on the site, which you can see in the following figure.

By the Way:

The IBA's site can be viewed two ways, using Shockwave or not. Shockwave is a freeware program that allows a multi-media presentation. It's a quick download, and I recommend using it because it adds to many sites, not just this one. The main page at *www. baseball.ch* allows you to select whether you want to enter the Shockwave site or the non-Shockwave site.

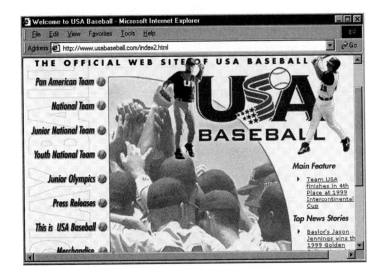

Other Countries' Organizations

Other countries also have organizations/federations/associations that govern baseball. Here's a quick look at a couple:

- **British Baseball Federation** You can follow the progress of British national teams at this site (*www.bbf.org*).

- **Baseball Canada** This is a very thorough site that offers a great deal of information on national teams and baseball in Canada in general. The main home page (*www.baseball.ca*) allows you to choose between the English- and French-language versions of the site (the English version can be seen in the following figure).

Baseball Canada offers thorough coverage of the game north of the border.

Rounding the Bases

Depending on how you look at the phrase "international baseball," there are a couple of different ways to go after the subject. You can cover international baseball competitions, like the Olympics, or you can cover baseball in other nations.

In this chapter, we attempted to do both.

There are a lot more international baseball resources than we covered here. It just might take some searching for you to find what you are looking for. Here's what we covered:

- Where to find information about Japanese professional baseball in the English language.

- How to locate Olympic baseball sites for both the Games in general and the U.S. team in particular.

- Sources of information about international competitions and U.S. national teams at various levels.

- Where to find information about other countries' national programs.

PART IV

A League of Your Own

CHAPTER 12

Playing in an Online Fantasy League

You can see it all the time. You're sitting at the ballpark watching a major-league game, and there's a guy there who's cheering for the home team. However, when a certain player on the other team hits a homer, this fan is actually *happy*.

Why?

That player is probably on his fantasy or rotisserie baseball team.

Some fans don't like that conflict of interest and avoid the games for that reason. But fantasy baseball is, by and large, a hobby that only serves to increase interest in the real games, and Major League Baseball in general.

For years, many baseball fans have sought out ways to get more involved in the game. Those who wanted to take on the role of owner, general manager, or manager would buy a baseball simulation board game like Strat-O-Matic and play games at home for hours.

Those board games were always based on statistics generated in previous seasons, however. For many baseball fans, that simply wasn't good enough.

So they invented a way of playing a simulated game that used statistics from the current season. It eliminated the roll of the dice and replaced it with a little bit more reality.

People have been playing in fantasy sports leagues for many years now, and it's believed that it was baseball fans that got the whole craze started. Now, of course, the football folks have gone crazy and there are also fantasy leagues for other sports such as basketball, hockey, auto racing, golf, and so on.

What You'll Learn in This Chapter:

▶ How fantasy leagues work, including the difference between "fantasy" and "rotisserie" baseball leagues.

▶ Where you can find leagues on the Internet in which you can participate.

▶ How you manipulate your team in an online fantasy baseball league.

▶ How you can use the Internet to prepare for your league's draft or player auction.

▶ How you can use Internet services to help you once your league is up and running.

By the Way:

Baseball simulation board games are now being played on computer, and leagues exist over the Internet. That topic is covered in Chapter 14, "Computer Baseball Games."

By the Way:

A little forewarning here: The vast majority of fantasy leagues that are played online require an entry fee of some sort. Some give out small prizes, such as a t-shirt, to league winners and even nicer prizes such as cruises to the top teams in all of the leagues combined. But you should be aware that there is a fee involved in most of these leagues, and should take that into account when deciding which service's league you would like to join.

The craze has spawned a whole new niche industry of magazine publishers and radio talk-show hosts and Internet sites that support people who are involved in it.

In this chapter, we'll get into the basics of fantasy leagues and how you can get involved in one over the Internet.

How Fantasy/Rotisserie Leagues Work

Before you can truly understand how online fantasy leagues are set up, you need to see how they were set up before the Internet joined the mainstream.

Typically, a group of friends get together to form a league of eight to 12 teams. Each person in the league owns a "franchise" and generally pays an entry fee to get into the league.

Usually, one of the owners is the league's "commissioner," or the person who is responsible for creating and upholding the rules of the league. The commissioner also keeps track of the rosters and so on.

By the Way:

If you are a fantasy-league veteran, you can probably avoid this section of the chapter.

In baseball, because there are so many statistics to track and games are played every day, leagues often contract with a statistics service to provide the stats for the league. Either that, or they compensate the commissioner or another league owner for handling the stats.

The league holds a draft or player auction, at which teams fill out their rosters. Rosters are made up of real major-league players—some leagues are American League only, some are National League only, and some use players from both leagues.

Rosters include players from all positions, so that you can field a team of players. Franchise owners set their starting lineups, and those players' statistics count toward league results.

Fantasy or Rotisserie?

You'll hear baseball hobbyists saying either "fantasy" or "rotisserie," but the terms are not interchangeable. In fact, they are completely different types of leagues.

In a rotisserie league, hitters and pitchers accumulate stats over a period of time in certain statistical categories. Hitters are usually graded on batting averages, home runs, RBIs, and stolen bases, which pitchers are tracked for their earned run averages, saves, wins, hits, and walks per nine innings. (These categories may vary.) All of a team's pitchers and all of its hitters are grouped together to get team totals in these categories, and teams earn points based on their standing in the league. For example, the team with the highest batting average in an eight-team league gets eight points, the second-best average would get seven points, and so on. The same is done for every statistical category. Whichever team has the most total points at the end of the season is the league champion.

In a fantasy league, teams play games against each other. Players earn points based on their performance. For example, a player might get two points for a hit, four for a home run, and one for each RBI and stolen base they have in a game. Pitchers might get 10 points for a win and one for every strikeout, and so on. Players' stats over a specified period of time, such as a week, are added together to create a team's total score. That score is compared to his opponent's score to determine the winner. In fantasy games, standings are kept, just like in the big leagues.

Originally, most baseball leagues were rotisserie leagues, but now fantasy leagues are gaining in popularity.

If you're going to play in an online fantasy or rotisserie league, you are going to want to carefully read the rules. Typically, these rules are very long, but without a good understanding of them, you'll be in for a long season. For example, if you don't know when you can make a roster move or if those roster moves are free, it can hurt your chances of having a successful season.

Any decent fantasy-league Web site is going to have a rules page or pages. ESPN.com offers fantasy leagues in a wide variety of sports, including baseball. The folks at ESPN haven't missed a beat in providing various sets of rules for prospective owners. Better yet, they let you read the complete rules *before* you join the league—which is something some sites don't let you do.

Let's take a walk through the ESPN site and find the rules for the fantasy baseball league they offer.

▼ **Try It Yourself**

1. Go to the main ESPN Web site at *http://espn.go.com* and click on the Fantasy Games link in the menu on the left side of the screen (you have to scroll down a ways).

2. Under the ESPN Fantasy Games header, click the Baseball button.

3. You will go to the main Fantasy Baseball home page. On the left is a menu of links. Click the Rules link.

▲

4. You will find the Rules Index, as you can see in the following figure. Just click any subject header to read that portion of the rules. It's that easy!

ESPN.com's fantasy baseball site offers complete rules for players.

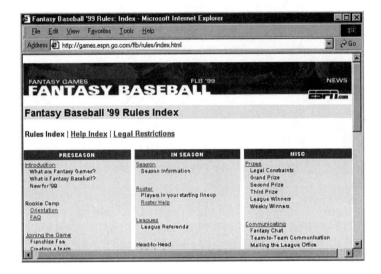

Finding a League to Join

Once you've decided to play in a fantasy or rotisserie baseball league, finding one to join is about as tough as catching a lazy fly ball.

Here's the Scoop:

You can also play on the Internet against your friends, relatives, and co-workers. That's covered in chapter 13, "Starting Your Own League Online."

Fantasy baseball leagues, once only the bastion of neighborhood and workplace settings, are now everywhere on the Internet. Instead of playing against friends, relatives, or co-workers, you can play against complete strangers if you want.

Anybody who's anybody in the sports world offers some form of fantasy games for its online users. Everyone from The Sporting News to ESPN to CNN/Sports Illustrated offer fantasy games with varying costs, rules, and competitive levels. Even organizations not typically identified with sports—such as Yahoo!—offer fantasy leagues in various sports, including baseball.

Any of the above-mentioned outlets are good places to go for fantasy- or rotisserie-league play. But let's take a look at some other sources that specialize in fantasy sports for serious fans.

Neyer's Nugget: Free Fantasies?

As Bob Temple points out, *most* Internet fantasy leagues will cost you, although the fee is generally moderate. There *are* free leagues out there, but you might want to think long and hard before joining one of them—unless you've got a group of friends to fill out your league. Why? Because when it's free, people tend to sign up for multiple teams and then quickly lose interest in the teams that don't perform well. So even if you win your league, where's the fun if nobody else is trying? As it turns out, most quality services have discovered that customer satisfaction actually goes up when there's at least a nominal charge for joining a fantasy league.

Now, which fantasy league to join? Although it's a bit pricey, I recommend Bill James Fantasy Baseball, available through STATS, Inc. at *www.stats.com*. The problem with most fantasy and rotisserie leagues is that they bear little relation to the actual sport because the scoring rules are so simplistic. In "straight" rotisserie, for example, a player who steals a lot of bases is extremely valuable, even if he has no other talents. A pitcher who racks up a lot of saves is also extremely valuable, even if his ERA sounds like Boeing built it.

Bill James Fantasy Baseball is different. The rules include a multitude of scoring categories—even double plays turned for middle infielders, and runners caught stealing for catchers—and the rosters must be constructed much like real teams. As James recently told me, "I wanted to have a game in which the value of the players matched their real-life value, as nearly as possible, rather than a game in which the values of certain players was exaggerated because they helped you in certain categories or because they qualified for certain positions due to holes in the position limits."

James succeeded. His league isn't cheap, and it isn't simple, but if it's realism you're after, nothing beats BJFB. (In the interest of full disclosure, let me say that I was working for Bill when he invented the game, and I later spent a couple of years working for STATS, Inc. That was a long time ago, though, and I still think it's the best game out there.)

Baseball Manager

Baseball Manager is a fantasy-style baseball game for Internet users. The Web site can be found at *www.baseballmanager.com*, and it can be seen in the following figure.

There are three different games that can be played, ranging from a 162-game schedule to a 54-game "Lightning" season. All leagues offer head-to-head play.

Baseball Manager uses its own scoring system to determine winners in each night's games. Unlike many fantasy games, you are given a salary budget with which to work, making it more like the real game.

Baseball Manager offers three different styles of play.

One Man's Opinion:
Of course, the "real" game also features teams like the Yankees and Dodgers, who don't seem to need to worry about a budget at all. So if you were George Steinbrenner or Rupert Murdoch, playing in one of these leagues might be a real challenge!

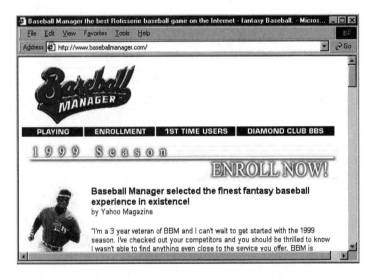

By the Way:
Setting pitching rotations and using different lineups for different days is a relatively new feature for fantasy baseball leagues, and it's added a lot of realism for fantasy players.

You can also set daily lineups and pitching rotations, so that you can match your lineup against your opponent in a way that is more like the real game.

Commissioner.com

Fantasy baseball at Commissioner.com can be played in four different ways—three rotisserie options and one head-to-head option.

You can check out these various options at the Commissioner.com Web site at *http://fantasybaseball.commissioner.com*. You can see the site in the following figure.

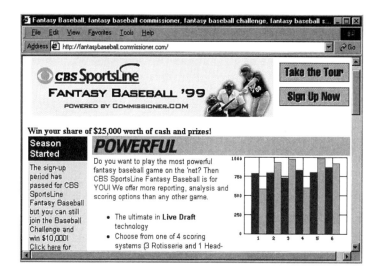

Owners can participate in a live draft at Commissioner.com.

As you can see from the figure, cash prizes are offered to the top owners in all of the leagues combined.

Commissioner.com offers a live draft, which is becoming more and more common in online fantasy leagues.

Live Draft Versus List Draft:

There are a wide variety of ways to build your roster. Different services offer different types of drafts.

In a live draft, selections are made in real time through a means similar to a chat room. You make your pick, and it appears on the screen for all the other owners to see.

In a list draft, you can rank your players by position, and a computer determines who you get. So, you might get your first choice at short-stop but you might get your ninth choice at first base, for example.

Both types have their merits, but if you have the time and your computer is up to the task, I suggest doing the live draft, because that's a big part of the fun of playing in a fantasy league.

Commissioner.com also offers a drag-and-drop interface for building your player list for a list draft, making it one of the easiest sites to use.

Small World Baseball

This is one of a couple of fantasy leagues that combines traditional fantasy play with a stock market-like factor that adds a little twist to the play.

The basic idea is this: Your team accumulates points for its play on the field, just like the other fantasy leagues. However, Small World sets a player's value based on how many teams in all of its leagues have that particular player on their roster.

You have a set budget to work with, but player values change every day. The idea, like the stock market, is to "buy" players at a low value and "sell" them when their value is high.

So, if you pick up a rookie valued at $250,000, and he gets hot at the start of the season, a lot of other teams are going to pick him up, too. That will drive his value up. And, if you think his value goes too high, you can drop him and pick up other players to replace him.

The Small World Baseball site can be found at *http://baseball.smallworld.com.*

Getting Ready for Your Draft and Playing in the League

You can't expect to have a very good fantasy or rotisserie team without doing some research to get ready for your draft. And the more closely you follow the game during the season, the better off you're going to be in your league.

Of course, one way to get ready for your draft is to simply be a fan of Major League Baseball. Reading your newspaper or checking out the latest news on the Web can only help you as a fantasy franchise owner.

Here's the Scoop:
Whether the league you play in is Internet-based or not, you can still use the Internet to gather information that will help you be a more effective owner!

But it helps a great deal if you can have a source or two that boils down the latest happenings for you from a fantasy sports perspective.

There are a lot of sources you can turn to. A lot of the major media outlets that offer fantasy sports online will also have a fantasy columnist or even a staff of writers who report on fantasy-related news. There are also some Web sites that are designed specifically to provide information for the fantasy owner.

Some are better than others. Here's a look at a few different sites that can help you as a fantasy baseball franchise owner.

USA Today's Rotisserie Corner

USA Today is, of course, a great source of information for fantasy baseball players in and of itself. But the newspaper's online edition also offers a special site just for the fantasy baseball player.

Rotisserie Corner, as you can see in the following figure, is full of resources for players. You can view it for yourself at *www.usatoday.com/sports/baseball/rotisix.htm.*

One fear that all fantasy players have, regardless of the sport they play in, is that they won't know about an injury to one of their players. Rotisserie Corner offers full injury reports on a daily basis to prevent this from happening.

In addition, you can get information about matchups, probable starting pitchers, and follow the trends through a couple of different columns devoted to fantasy baseball.

USA Today's Rotisserie Corner is jam-packed with information for fantasy players.

RotoNews

RotoNews' baseball site offers a ton of information, and does an especially good job of helping you get ready for the start of your season.

Visit this site (*www.rotonews.com/baseball/*) and get complete player rankings at every position, in addition to predictions for the upcoming season. Check it out in the following figure.

RotoNews also goes beyond the major-league regulars to keep an eye on prospects that might be able to make an impact on a roster in the coming season. Those players can be great late-round draft picks or low-money auction purchases that make the difference between a good fantasy season and a bad one.

By the Way:

Some fantasy leagues have "minor leagues" in which each owner has the rights to a certain number of players who are not in the majors. If that's the case in your league, using a Web site like RotoNews can help you find these sleepers who will make an impact for you at a later date.

RotoJunkie

RotoJunkie bills itself as "your daily rotisserie fix," and it provides that and more. You can visit the site at *www.rotojunkie.com*, and you can see it in the following figure.

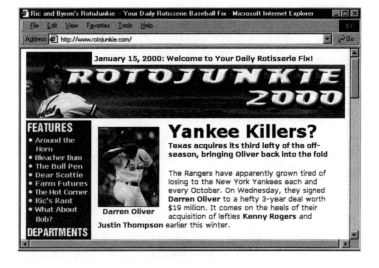

This site can be described as rotisserie information with an attitude, as the information is presented in a less-than-objective style.

Like some other fantasy information sites, this one offers a message board (called "The Bullpen") that allows users of the site to share information and opinions about players, and so on.

Rounding the Bases

This chapter laid the groundwork for getting involved in a fantasy or rotisserie baseball league. By this point, you should know:

- How fantasy and rotisserie baseball leagues work.

- How to find the rules for an online fantasy league.

- Where to find online leagues in which you can play.

- Where you can go on the Internet for information that will help prepare for the start of your season and keep you ahead of the pack during the season.

CHAPTER 13

Starting Your Own League Online

Playing fantasy baseball is a lot of fun, period. But depending on your perspective, certain leagues can be more fun than others.

In the previous chapter, we covered how fantasy leagues are set up and how you can get involved in them online. Those leagues, as we discussed them in that chapter, typically involve people from around the country (the world, even) that you do not know.

You are competing for pride and for the fun of it and, in some cases, for prizes.

There's nothing quite like competing for *bragging rights*. That's what makes playing in a league with friends, relatives, and co-workers such fun. When it's all said and done, if you're the champion, you've got bragging rights until the next season rolls around.

What's funny is that a lot of fantasy baseball players think that the choices are this simple—play with strangers on the Internet or play with friends. They don't realize that one of the best ways to participate in a fantasy league is to combine the best of both of those options. You can play in a league with people you know and use the Internet to do it, even if you all work in the same office.

Why not just pass out a stat sheet to everybody if you're so close, you ask? Simple. Using the Internet opens up other possibilities, like using an online stat service or commissioner service that keeps all the mundane work out of the league so you can concentrate on the fun.

And, even if you aren't going to use an Internet-based stats service, you can still post your league's news and stats on the Internet for team owners to read. It's just more convenient, and often less costly, than mailing out weekly newsletters.

What You'll Learn in This Chapter:

▶ How you use the services of one of the major fantasy-league sites to host your private league.

▶ Where you can find a commissioner service online to facilitate your league.

▶ How Internet-based statistics services allow you to use the Internet without putting your entire league online.

▶ How you can use the Internet to better communicate with other owners in your league, regardless of who does your stats or is your commissioner.

By the Way:

There are other reasons, too. For one thing, many employers want this type of stuff kept out of the office. (If you keep it on the Web, the boss will never know.)

One Man's Opinion:

I've played in leagues both ways—with friends and with strangers on the Internet. They both have their merits. I had great fun the year I got involved, quite accidentally, with a group of know-it-all students from an Ivy League college. Winning that league was fun, but I haven't come in contact with any of them since. When you win a league against friends, you've got a title you can brag about forever.

By the Way:

I'm involved in one league that includes friends who live in different parts of the country. Most of us are in the Minneapolis area, but one lives in Detroit and another in New York. Using the Internet evens the playing field; everybody submits lineups and transactions by email so that no one has long-distance charges, and then everyone can get the weekly league "mailing" at the same time.

That's what this chapter is all about. Instead of learning about how to participate in *someone else's* league, we're going to talk about bringing your league into the 21st Century by getting it up on the Web. Or, if you're considering starting a league for the first time, you'll get some helpful information about that, too.

A Private League in a Public Place

There are many levels to being part of a rotisserie or fantasy baseball league. At the highest level is the commissioner, or whatever you choose to call the person who coordinates the league's functions.

That job can be exceedingly difficult or very, very easy, depending on how you go about it (see the sidebar titled "The Role of the Commissioner"). How much the rest of the owners in a league agree to fork out in terms of cash also makes a difference.

The Role of the Commissioner:

Depending on how your league is (or is going to be) set up, the role of the commissioner can be very different. Some leagues have a number of different people carrying out commissioner duties, while others are run as more of a monarchy.

Regardless, *someone* has to carry out these duties. The commissioner generally oversees the draft, keeps track of team rosters (including transactions and trades) throughout the season, records starting lineups, keeps track of standings statistics and the results of games (if a fantasy league), keeps the league standings up to date, and resolves any disputes between owners.

It's a lot of work, especially in a baseball league, because games are played every day and there are a lot of statistics to keep.

Using the Internet for your fantasy league can make the commissioner's job much, much easier. Depending on how you go about it and which services you use, you can have an Internet-based entity take on part of your league or run the whole darn thing for you.

Since online fantasy league organizers can probably provide accurate stats more quickly that you can, it might just be to the benefit of the entire league, not just the commissioner, to move onto the Internet.

It's not just about whether you want your league to be "cool" and have a Web site. Most leagues find they actually are better organized when they move to the Internet.

Using ESPN.com to "Run" Your Fantasy League

As discussed in Chapter 12, ESPN.com offers fantasy leagues for its users. For a small fee, ESPN sets up the leagues and runs them.

ESPN's leagues can be "public" or "private." In a public league, you are matched up against other players from around the globe. You can have some control over who you play against, because you can pick the league that you enter. But in many cases, you end up being dropped into a league with people you have never met before.

A private league allows you to determine who can play with you. This is the means you should use if you want to move your existing league onto the Internet (or start a new one there).

When you set up the league as "private," you create a password that allows only the people you want in the league to join. You tell the other owners in the league the name you gave the league and the password, and they sign up with ESPN.com using the same information.

The major drawback to this type of setup is that you are forced to use ESPN's rules for playing the game. There are several choices for how the league is set up, but any quirky rules that your league might have had are generally out the window. Because of that, this type of service works best with a league that is just forming, rather than an already-established league.

Also, ESPN requires 10 teams per league, so if your league has more teams, this won't work. And, if you end up with fewer than 10, other teams will be added in to fill out the league.

If you didn't bookmark the ESPN fantasy baseball site last chapter, the best way to get there is to go to *espn.go.com*, click on the Fantasy Games link in the menu on the left, then click the Baseball button on the top of the Fantasy Games page. You can see the page in the following figure.

By the Way:

You don't have to use an Internet service for *all* of the commissioner's duties. Some services just offer statkeeping for fantasy leagues, but allow you to do the roster manipulation, and so on, that comes with being commissioner. This type of Internet usage is covered later in this chapter.

By the Way:

There are other fantasy-league operators who allow you to set up private leagues in their service. This is just one example.

ESPN hosts "private" fantasy leagues so you can determine whom you play against.

Renting a Commissioner at Commissioner.com

If your league is already established and you are looking for an online service to run it *your* way, then you need to go shopping for an e-commissioner.

It just so happens that one exists at Commissioner.com. Their baseball site is available at *baseball.commissioner.com*, and you can see it in the following figure.

Commissioner.com offers a lot of setup options.

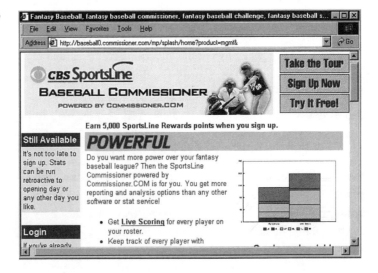

Because Commissioner.com is set up to be a commissioner service rather than to operate its own leagues (primarily, at least), it offers a lot more setup options for existing leagues.

First of all, you can choose between a fantasy and rotisserie format. You can set your own schedule of games, rather than having the computer do it for you. You can determine which teams are in which divisions, and so on.

There are, of course, limitations (there are limitations with anything). But the choices available through Commissioner.com make it likely that your existing league can use the service without too many changes in the way you do business.

And you'll probably find that things are even better online. Commissioner.com offers a chat room just for your league's owners, and customizable reports that allow each owner to determine what they would like to see.

Using a Statistics Service

Some leagues want more local control. Heck, the reason you set up the league your way in the first place was so you could control how it functions.

These leagues often run independently for football, because the stat-keeping is reduced to just the weekends (and Monday night). But in the other sports (especially baseball, when there is often 15 major-league games in a night), keeping up with the stats on your own can be a very difficult enterprise.

That's where a stats service comes into play. Using their software and a link to the Internet, you can download stats from a service's Web page quickly and easily, whenever you want them. Then, you import them into the software for handling the league and—presto!—you've got your reports ready to be printed.

One such service is Spin Stats, Inc. For a small fee, you buy their software, which you use to set up and run your league. It offers tons of variations on how you play, from fantasy to rotisserie to a wide variety of scoring systems.

You still retain total control over when roster changes can be made, and you make them, not the computer. Then, you go to their Web page (*www.spinstats.com*) and download the stats, whenever you need them. Check out the following figure to see the site.

Spin Stats is one of a number of statistics services on the Internet.

One Man's Opinion:

I have run both baseball and basketball leagues using outside statistics providers for stat updates. Once you learn the software, which is usually very user-friendly, running the league this way is a snap. You retain a lot of control, but don't have to worry about the biggest headache of all, the stats. So if you're not ready to turn all the work over to an online commissioner service, this is the way to go.

Like other stats services, Spin Stats updates the statistics daily. That's important, because not all leagues run their reporting schedules from Monday-Sunday. By updating the stats daily, you can pick when you need to download stats.

The biggest drawback to this type of service is that it requires you to use (and learn) their software. But you would have some up-front learning to do regardless of what level of Internet service you used.

Communicating Within Your League Online

Even if you don't use the Internet in any of the above ways for your league, you can still use the Web as a communication tool for your league.

Most "traditional" fantasy or rotisserie leagues send out some type of weekly or biweekly mailing to the participants in the league with stats, standings, and some type of weekly recap.

This can get to be a pain, especially when you consider all the printing and copying and mailing that goes into it. There is a better way, so long as all the owners in your league are online. You can set up a Web site (for a very minimal cost—see "A Word About Cost") for your league and publish your updates online!

A Word About Cost:

Setting up a Web site just for the sake of supporting your fantasy sports habit might seem a little excessive at first glance. But you don't have to have a professionally designed site, and there can actually be a cost benefit.

If you send a weekly update to 11 owners for the entire baseball season, you can easily spend $100 on stamps, envelopes and paper, not to mention ink for your printer or the cost of photocopies.

Since most popular word processing and spreadsheet programs offer you the ability to convert your files to HTML (Microsoft Office applications do), many people already have the ability to create Web pages, whether they know it or not.

You'll also need space on an ISP's server, but most (including America Online) offer up to 5 MB of space free of charge with your dialup account.

So using the Web can actually be a money-saver for your league, allowing you to keep entry fees lower or to pay out more to winners at the end of the season!

The important thing to remember is that your site doesn't have to be fancy. Since the audience is 10–16 people, you can be pretty straightforward. Now, if you happen to have a copy of a Web-design software program and know your way around design a little, you can do more, like the members of Boulder Valley League Baseball (see the following figure).

This is an example of a private fantasy league using the Internet to provide information to owners.

Their site (*fm220.Colorado.edu/~coyle/Baseball.html*) includes a very humorous Preamble to their "constitution" and results for every year the league has existed. It's just one example of a site that can be created for a private league.

Even if you don't want to go to the trouble of setting up a Web page (it's not that much trouble), you can still use the online environment to communicate within your league. Just send out your reports to the owners via email and they can print them out themselves! (You will need to make sure that they have the same program that you do.)

Rounding the Bases

This chapter was devoted to the fantasy league owner (especially the commissioner) who wants to use the Internet to simplify the running of the league. We've shown that the Internet can be used to completely run the league or just for the basics dissemination of information.

We covered:

• Using a Web-based service to run your league from top to bottom.

• Using a statistics service to handle just the numbers portion of running a fantasy baseball league.

• Using the Web to create your own basic site for your private league.

CHAPTER 14

Computer Baseball Games

The previous two chapters have covered fantasy and rotisserie baseball. These are both wonderful pastimes that allow everyday folks like me to control a pseudo major-league team.

There's another type of baseball simulation out there that goes about the same thing in a very different way—computer games.

Now, we're not talking about the Nintendo or Sega games that use arcade skills to produce results. While those games may allow you to use "real" major league players, we're not going to cover the games that test your thumb speed more than your baseball knowledge.

We're talking about baseball *strategy* games that test your knowledge of the game and how to use players to their maximum effectiveness.

Many of these games started out as tabletop board games in the era before the computer took over our lives, and have since evolved into a computer version of the game. Others are straight PC or Internet creations. They each have their own merits, but a few things are similar.

First, they are based on *past* performance of major-league players. Typically, when you are playing the 2000 season using the latest version of one of these games, it will be based on the performance of the players from the 1999 season. This (and other differences) from fantasy baseball has created a fissure between the proponents of the various types of games (see the sidebar called "The Great Debate").

The Great Debate:

Fantasy versus simulation. It all depends on your personal preferences.

Fantasy gives you the realism of today's performances. While it allows you to set rosters, make trades, and so on, it doesn't allow you the in-game management options.

Simulation games don't reflect current performance of players but they do allow you to act as a manager on the field, making changes batter by batter. They also allow you to use players from different eras in the same game.

So which is better? Who knows? My personal preference—I like 'em both!

So, how does the Internet come into play here? In some cases, these games can be played against other players over a live Internet connection. There are some companies that set up leagues, just like the fantasy leagues, only they use simulation games instead. Others are leagues set up with friends that use the Internet to post results and standings to the rest of the league.

In this chapter, we'll look at computer baseball games on the Internet, and how you can participate or use the Internet to further your existing hobby.

Board Games on the Web

Ah, my old baseball board games. I've tried about 10 different companies' simulation games, and I don't think I've found one yet that I didn't love.

In my youth (insert your own age joke here), I would spend hours sitting in my room, rolling dice and checking player cards, then carefully recording the results of every play. Once the games were over, I'd record the stats by hand on my notebook pages, keeping each team in my solitaire league up-to-date.

Looking back on it today it almost sounds like a pain in the neck. But I have nothing but fond memories of that time and those games.

Today, those same games still exist. You can still get the tabletop version of just about all of them. Most of them have computerized versions, too.

The computerized versions do lack some of the romanticism of the board versions, but they have also improved the realism of the games.

When a person has to look up results of a dice roll on a chart or player card, you have a finite number of options that can take place. But when you have use of a computer's microprocessor to determine the various potential results, the game comes to life.

The best part, for those of us who have done it the other way, is that most of these games keep all the stats up-to-date for you, so you don't have to mess around with them yourself.

What a relief.

Some people who play the computerized versions of board games play them in leagues made up of people from all over the country. They've developed a way to play them long-distance, and they use the Internet to communicate results.

Let's take a look at a couple of the longest-running board games and how computers and the Internet now interact with them.

Ordering Games and Interacting with the Makers

One way in which computer "board" game companies use the Internet is, of course, as a marketing tool. You can order just about any simulation game on the Web.

You can also use the Internet to interact with the manufacturer of the game; many offer FAQs and email addresses for questions or other types of tech support. You might even find a chat room on the site for users of the game.

Strat-O-Matic has been selling games for a variety of different sports since 1960. Baseball lends itself to this type of game better than any other sport, because the one-on-one pitcher-on-batter matchup is the start of everything that happens in a baseball game.

Strat-O-Matic offers a computer version of the game. It is not a computer baseball game, per se. Instead, it is more an extension of the board game, just offered to you through your computer. You can use the computer for stats and to handle the processing of the game all you want.

If you wish, however, you can still roll the dice on your desktop and input the result into the game (a feature that Strat-O-Matic traditionalists really love).

Whether you want the original board game, the computer version, or another product, one way these companies use the Internet is to allow online ordering.

The Strat-O-Matic Game Company has been in business since 1960.

The Strat-O-Matic Web site (*www.strat-o-matic.com*) offers online ordering, fixes, and patches for its computer games—even tech support. You can see the site in the following figure.

Playing Leagues on the Web

Some computer "board" game players go so far as to set up online leagues with people from around the country.

Typically, the game must be played at one person's location or the other, so the person on whose computer the game is played has more direct impact on the play. He or she can directly make lineup changes and strategic moves.

The other player is not present, and so must relinquish control of his team to the game's computer manager. He usually will specify

settings for the computer manager, such as when to bunt, whom
to pinch-hit for and when, and so on. Unfortunately, he doesn't
have the direct impact on the game that the other player has. It's a
distinct home-field advantage.

That is, of course, unless the game is played using the Internet.
Some leagues will go so far as to set up chat rooms in which two
owners playing against each other can engage in a long-distance
game of, say, APBA Baseball.

This way, one owner actually is playing the game on his computer, and he communicates what is happening through the chat
room to the other player. The long-distance player then tells the
other player what to do as the game goes along.

APBA Baseball has been played since 1951, and there are some
leagues around the country that have existed for about that long.
Many of those leagues have moved their information and league
organizational materials to the Internet.

The Twentieth Century Baseball Association is a group of APBA-
based leagues that replay major-league seasons from a variety of
eras. You can see this group's Web site at *www.geocities.com/
Colosseum/3211/* (and in the following figure).

This site offers an attractive front page and it's text-based on the
inside. It's a great example that shows that you don't have to go
to extremes just to have a Web site. As long as it serves its purpose—to serve league owners, in this case—then its job is done.

If you are blessed enough to have someone in your league (or
running your league) who is a Web designer, however, you *can* go
to extremes and have a lot of fun doing it.

Take the North American Strat-O-Matic Baseball League, for
example. Coverage of the league on its Web site (*www.nasbl.com*)
rivals coverage of the major leagues provided by national media
outlets. Check out the Web site in the following figure.

The teams in the league even have email addresses using the
league's domain. It really adds to the enjoyment of playing in a
league when you can add a great Web site to it.

By the Way:

There are some com-
puter games that
can be played live, in
real time, over the
Internet with both
players interacting
with the game.
Usually, these are
games that were
designed specifically
for the computer,
rather than being
converted board
games. You'll find an
example in the next
section of this chap-
ter.

By the Way:

Another aspect of
simulation games
that is attractive to
fans is that you can
use players from dif-
ferent eras. You can
recreate your youth
by using players you
loved as a child, and
can even mix them
in with players who
are playing today.
So, for example, you
could have a team
with Lou Gehrig,
Willie Mays, and
Ken Griffey, Jr. all
playing together!

This APBA-based league has its own site on the Web.

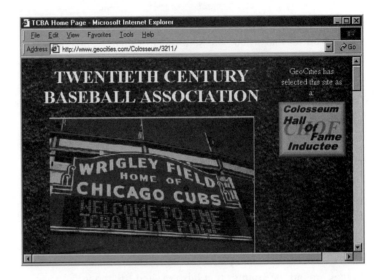

This Strat-O-Matic league's site covers the league like the big media outlets.

By the Way:
There are dozens of these types of games on the market, and this section—this entire book, in fact—is not intending to endorse one over any others. They all have their advantages, and only you can determine which game will be the most enjoyable for *you*.

Computer Games Use the Internet, Too

The previous section covered baseball games that started on the tabletop and moved into cyberspace. What about the games that actually started as computer simulations?

Again, these aren't the games in which you "swing" the bat for the batter—the arcade-style games; these are strategy-based games.

One of the top computer games is Diamond Mind Baseball, and it is also one of the few that allows you to play the game live over the Internet using a program such as Microsoft NetMeeting or PCAnywhere.

You can see the Web site at *www.diamond-mind.com.*

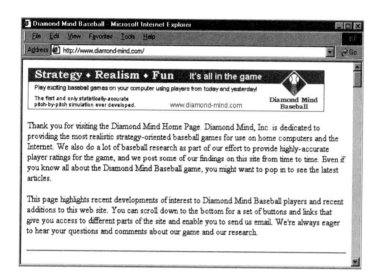

Diamond Mind allows you to play live over the Internet.

Diamond Mind lets you to determine how you want to pitch to each batter. For example, if first base is open and you're facing Mark McGwire with two outs, you might want to pitch around him or issue an intentional walk. It also gives you a pitch-by-pitch simulation.

The ability to play the game live over the Internet is a great advantage. But remember: It does require knowledge of another program.

Neyer's Nuggets

Neyer's Nugget: Baseball in Print and Out of Print

One of the wonderful things about the Internet is the relative ease of acquiring books, whether they're in print or not. Books in print can easily be ordered from sellers of new books such as Barnes & Noble or Amazon.com. Out-of-print books can also often be ordered from those sites, or from

continues

continued

used-book clearinghouses such as Alibris.com
(*www.alibris.com*). And of course, auction sites such as eBay
are also great sources for old books. Given the agility of the
Internet, there's never been a better time to build a baseball
library. Below are ten non-fiction volumes that I consider
essential in any such library.

Babe, by Robert Creamer
Baseball's greatest player and greatest character deserves a
great biography, and this is the one. Creamer's research is
solid and, just as important, he writes beautifully.

Ball Four, by Jim Bouton
The funniest non-fiction baseball book, and there's not
really any competition. No self-respecting baseball fan
should go through life without reading *Ball Four* at least
three times. In this volume, knuckleballer Bouton chronicles
his 1969 struggles while pitching for the Seattle Pilots.

The Bill James Historical Baseball Abstract, by Bill James
This is really two books in one, with a decade-by-decade
look at the game and a section rating the all-time greats at
each position. The 1986 edition is long out of print, but an
update is scheduled for publication sometime in the next
year or so. In the meantime, James's recent books on the
Hall of Fame and managers are both excellent.

Bums: An Oral History of the Brooklyn Dodgers, by Peter
Golenbock
Golenbock's stories of Branch Rickey, Jackie Robinson, and
all the rest—largely related by the men who were there—
are fascinating. This might be the first book to give voice to
a team's fans. *Bums* was the first adult baseball book I read,
and it made me a true fan of baseball's wonderfully rich history.

The Glory of Their Times, edited by Lawrence Ritter
Many aficionados regard *The Glory of Their Times* as *the*
greatest baseball book. It was essentially the first of the
oral-history genre, and it remains the best. It's a wonderful
portrait of baseball in the first 20 years of this century.

Veeck as in Wreck, by Bill Veeck with Ed Linn
Baseball's greatest impresario, Bill Veeck, was also one of
the game's greatest storytellers. Add collaborator Ed Linn
to the equation, and you've got one of sport's best
autobiographies.

Once More Around the Park, by Roger Angell
If you don't feel like tracking down Angell's four earlier col-
lections of his baseball pieces from *The New Yorker* (*The
Summer Game, Five Seasons, Late Innings,* and *Season
Ticket)*, this retrospective is the next best thing. Angell is
easily baseball's most literate writer.

The Pitch That Killed, by Mike Sowell
A wonderful account of the 1920 American League cam-
paign, which included the breaking of the Black Sox scandal,
Babe Ruth's first truly historic season, and the fatal beaning
of Indians shortstop Ray Chapman. Although it's out of
print, you can still find the paperback edition floating
around in some bookstores.

Total Baseball, edited by John Thorn, Pete Palmer, et al.
More than a decade ago, *Total Baseball* supplanted
Macmillan's *Baseball Encyclopedia* as the best source of his-
torical data, and Thorn and Palmer are still going strong.
Internet statistical resources are wonderful, but sometimes
you want seven pounds of paper on your lap.

The Ultimate Baseball Book, edited by Dan Okrent and
Harris Lewine
This large-format overview of the sport in the 20th century
has gorgeous photos—some of them huge—and fine essays.
There are a number of excellent picture-driven baseball
books, and this one's probably the best.

No, I haven't forgotten baseball fiction. Without going into
detail, you won't be disappointed by any of the five following novels: Eric Rolfe Greenberg's *The Celebrant*; Philip
Roth's *The Great American Novel*; Mark Harris' *The
Southpaw*; Robert Coover's *The Universal Baseball
Association, Inc.: J. Henry Waugh, Prop.*; and Ring Lardner's
classic, *You Know Me Al*.

Joining an Online Gaming League

So far, you've read about leagues that *use* the Internet in one way
or another. Some use it as a communication tool within the league
by providing a Web site for league members. Some you can play
over the Internet using another piece of software.

Now, let's take a look at leagues and games that are actually
based on the Internet. The difference may seem subtle, but it isn't.

Playing in an online simulation league is closer to fantasy or rotisserie than the previously discussed types of gaming, in that you rarely have the batter-by-batter control that you do in the other games.

However, you can have a lot more control than you do in fantasy sports, and you can use players from eras other than the one in which we currently live.

By the Way:

Before you can play Diamond Legends, you might want to become a member of STATS, Inc. There is no cost to join, and it's as simple a process as picking a username and password. There is, of course, a cost to play Diamond Legends.

One such example is the Diamond Legends game offered by STATS, Inc. The Web site is at *www.stats.com.*

Playing Diamond Legends is very much like playing in a fantasy league provided by an Internet-based service. You draft your players and play generally against other people you do not know.

But the game itself is a simulation, and it's up to you to determine your starting pitching rotation, when to use relievers and whom to use, lefty and righty batting orders, pinch-hitter usage, and more.

Players from all eras are grouped together and given a "salary," and you are forced to work within a league-mandated salary cap.

You play a 162-game schedule over a nine-week period, so you play about three games a night. The results are ready for you first thing in the morning.

And, like the other simulation games, you can play it anytime you want, including in the dead of winter! STATS, Inc. is forming leagues all the time.

Use the following steps to take a quick tour of a sample Diamond Legends league.

Try It Yourself ▼

1. Go to the STATS, Inc., Web site at *www.stats.com.*

2. Click on the Diamond Legends link or logo to go to the main Diamond Legends page.

3. Scroll down the page and click on the Experience a Sample League link.

4. You'll get a page like the one in the following figure. You can click on any of the team names to see their rosters and stats or click any of the links on the left to view league reports.

▲

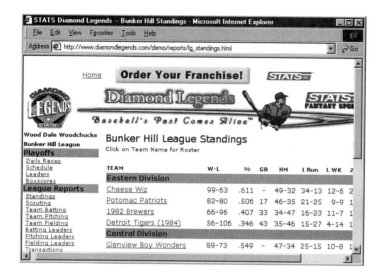

Diamond Legends is a true Internet-based simulation game.

Rounding the Bases

Simulation games are different from fantasy and rotisserie leagues in a number of ways, yet there are still some similarities. In this chapter, we looked at the various types of simulation games, including:

- How makers and players of games that began as board games now use the Internet and computers for those same games.

- How computer-based games have adapted to the Internet and allow users to play games against each other in real time.

- How fantasy and simulation games can come together to allow an Internet-based simulation game.

PART V

Extra Bases

CHAPTER 15

Collectibles and Memorabilia Online

So you're a baseball nut, huh? If it's got anything to do with the grand ol' game, you've probably got it sitting in a glass case in your den, right?

Well, do you have a replica 1986 World Series ring for the champion New York Mets like the ones that were given out at the ballpark early in 1987? Do you have a key chain commemorating the 1991 World Series champion Minnesota Twins?

What about a bobbing-head doll of Mark McGwire?

If you've got any of the above-listed items, I'm not sure if you are a baseball nut or just plain nuts. (I have one of them, but I'm not saying which.)

You might, instead, be spending your time on more mainstream collectibles. Baseball cards, of course, have been collected nationwide for about a century.

Regardless of what you collect or what type of memorabilia you fancy, having some of these items in your personal collection—of even just viewing them in someone else's—only adds to the fun of being a baseball fan.

So whether your idea of collecting memorabilia is your rack of hats from minor league teams or stacks and stacks of baseball cards gathering dust in an attic, it's all for the love of the game.

What You'll Learn in This Chapter:

▸ Where you can find the old standby, baseball cards, online.

▸ Some good sources for other collectibles, like game-worn jerseys.

▸ How to use the Internet to find some of the more odd collectibles, like the aforementioned bobbing-head dolls.

▸ How to use online auctions to find the collectible item you are looking for.

By the Way:
Depending on your
definition of "mem-
orabilia," you might
want to include
baseball books and
movies in it. We
don't. In fact, we've
separated those top-
ics out into their
own chapter, which
just happens to
come next. It's called
"Baseball in the
Arts," and it's chap-
ter 16.

Using the Internet for Baseball-card Collecting

Every spring, I'd wait impatiently for the first arrival of baseball
cards at the corner grocery store. When they finally came, I'd ride
up there on my bike and buy as many as my allowance—plus my
lawn-mowing money—would allow. Then I'd rush back home to
open them, and to chew the wonderful bubble gum that came with
them.

Baseball card collecting isn't what it used to be. The gum is gone,
the cards are gold-foiled or holographic or something, and they
cost a pretty penny. And, there are about 50 different printers of
baseball cards.

In many ways, baseball card collecting has lost some of its magic.
The cards are pricey enough now that a kid can hardly do what I
used to do with my cards, which was to play "Card Baseball"
with them (see the following sidebar).

But the success of the various card-makers tells a very clear story:
Collecting is still running strong, with no end in sight.

> **The Anatomy of Card Baseball:**
> Some kids put them in their bicycle spokes. Some kids played a game
> that involved flipping them. Some kids just sat down with friends and
> traded them.
>
> My brother and I played Card Baseball.
>
> It was a game we (mostly he) invented, in which you could use the cards
> and a die to play an actual game of baseball using the cards as players.
> There was an elaborate set of rules (of course).
>
> The players would run bases and chase after balls in the field based on
> the roll of the dice. A six, for example, meant the player could move six
> card-lengths closer to the next base. This, of course, involved folding the
> cards over and over, effectively wrecking them in the process.
>
> We couldn't have cared less.

Card Manufacturer's Web Sites

As each new set of cards hits the market each year, collectors of
all ages work diligently with one goal in mind: To get the complete set. Now, you can go out and just *buy* the complete set, but
that kind of spoils the fun.

What if you want to make sure you've got all the cards? You're going to need a checklist for that. You can go buy a collecting magazine to get the list of cards, or you can hop on the Web and print one out for free.

A good example is the Topps Web site at *www.topps.com*. Let's find a checklist series together.

1. Go to the Topps Web site at *www.topps.com*. Click on the Sports Trading Cards link.

2. On the Trading Cards page, click on the Baseball link.

3. You will see a list of card series, like in the following figure. Click on the series you want.

4. For many of the series, you can sort the list by card number, alphabetically, or by other means.

5. Print out the list you want, and start checking them off!

▼ **Try It Yourself**

▲

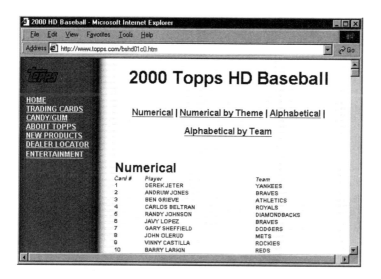

The Topps site offers checklists for the company's card series.

Finding Specific Cards Online

Serious collectors (and not-so-serious ones) generally have certain cards that are their favorites. Often, they also have a long-sought card that has somehow eluded their grasp.

There are umpteen sites that have been created by card dealers to sell their wares. And, there are just about as many sites on the

Web from collectors like you, looking to make a trade or two to fill out their collections.

If you're looking for a particular card, or card set, check out America's Pastime's Baseball Cards and Sports Autographs at *www.wwriches.com/ap/* (see the following figure).

This site offers cards for sale.

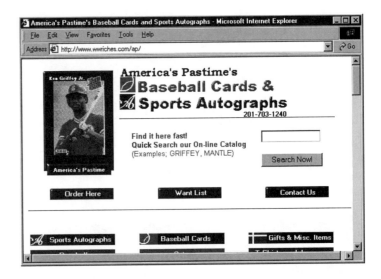

Much of the inventory is available on the site, but it would be virtually (pardon the pun) impossible to list it all. There's a button on the site called Want List, which you can use to go to a page where you can enter your contact information and a description of the specific item you seek.

Old-Time Cards on Display:

If you want to check out some *really* old baseball cards, check out the Library of Congress' online archive of cards produced from 1887-1914 (*www.memory.loc.gov/ammem/bbhtml/bbhome.html*).

You can see in the following figure that there's a very complete archive of cards there, and you can even order reproductions (although you can't buy the originals).

You can search the archive in a variety of ways. It's a great way to learn about the history of baseball cards, even if you can't hold them in your hot little hands.

Finding Other Baseball Memorabilia Online

There's a lot more to collecting than baseball cards, of course. There are many, many other things that baseball fans collect, from game-worn or game-used pieces to trinkets that might be given out at the games themselves.

For some people, it doesn't matter what the piece is; it only matters that it has something to do with the game of baseball. For others, collecting is a serious pursuit based on "filling out" a collection—making sure you've got every piece of the series.

Either way, it's fun.

Collecting the Equipment and Uniforms of the Pros

There's always been a market for pieces that have been a part of an actual game. It used to be that only the balls that went into the stands could be collected by fans.

Over time, though, a market developed for other game-used items, like bats, batting gloves, jerseys, even spikes. Get an autograph on it and it's worth even more.

There are many places on the Web from which you can purchase game-used apparel and equipment. Let's take a look at a couple that concentrate on this type of collectible.

Grey Flannel Collectibles specializes in game-worn uniforms, as you might have guessed. It goes well beyond baseball to other sports, but you can find some interesting baseball apparel at the site (*www.greyflannel.com*). You can see the site in the following figure.

Once you've got the jersey that you want all picked out, why not get a game-used bat to go with it?

You can find them at the BoomBats Web site at *www.boombats.com*. You can see it in the following figure.

This is a real piece of the action. Some of the bats might be cracked from their use in a game or batting practice, while others might have never been used by the player. Whatever the case, there's a full description of the bat and its condition.

A Word of Caution:
You should be careful when ordering online anything that claims to be game-used or game-worn. Since these items are typically very expensive, you should do your best to authenticate the piece before spending the money.

Grey Flannel Collectibles offers jerseys from professional players.

BoomBats offers bats that belonged to the pros.

Novelties and Other Collectible Items

The terms "memorabilia" and "collectibles" don't have to describe the kind of merchandise that a person would lock up in a display case forever. It doesn't have to be items you would trade with friends or a set you need to complete, either.

For some fans, collecting means getting anything and everything they can with their favorite team's logo on it. Some might buy a team cap or a replica jersey. Others might go for a coffee cup or a license plate holder or t-shirt.

It doesn't matter. These kinds of things are available all over the Internet.

One good place to start is an e-tailer called The Press Box (*www.shoppressbox.com*). You can see the Major League Baseball page at *www.shoppressbox.com/pressbox/mlb.com*, and in the following figure.

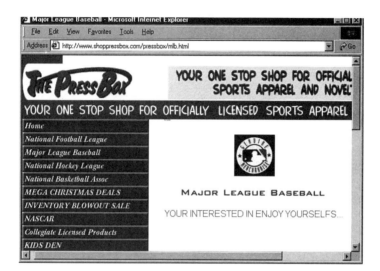

Novelties and other collectibles are available at The Press Box.

There are all kinds of "traditional" collectibles like autographed baseballs here, but you can also find other items as well. Everything from key chains to golf balls to teddy bears to duffle bags—all of them with the team logo—can be found here. Just give yourself plenty of time to shop.

Bobbing-Head Dolls

Years ago, they were a kitschy little novelty. Those little dolls with the boyish smiling face looking at you from the back of the car in front of you, their heads bobbing up and down.

Usually, they would be wearing the uniform of a major-league team.

For a long time, they seemed to be out of circulation. At least, they weren't *x*like they had been before. Then they showed up in a couple of ESPN's more offbeat commercials, and the next thing you know, you're starting to see them around again.

Guess what? You can find them on the Web, too. Bobble Dolls, Inc.'s Web site at *www.bobblehead.com* offers the "traditional" bobble-head doll—the one with that generic, boyish face as you can see in the following figure. Other sites also offer bobble-head dolls, but they have other features (see "Bobble-Headed Likenesses").

The original bob-ble-head doll can be found on the Web.

> **Bobble-Headed Likenesses:**
>
> As if getting a boyish-faced bobble-head doll isn't enough, you can even get a bobble head doll that is a likeness of one of your favorite players.
>
> Two different sites that I found offer bobble-heads of major leaguers. One of them, *www.sportbobbers.com*, offers bobbers of current and for-mer great major-league players. Another, *www.bobbing.com*, offers both bobbing head dolls and figurines of players in a number of differ-ent sports, including baseball.

Online Auctions

Just one of many of the latest rages in the online world are auc-tions. The popularity and success of eBay has made auctioning on the Internet commonplace.

There are many sites that offer auctioning as a sideline to their normal course of business, and there are plenty of others that are auction-only sites.

One of the former is the Sporting News' Web site, which offers auctions of sports memorabilia at *auctions.sportingnews.com*.

But the king of all auction sites, even those for sports memorabilia, is eBay. That popularity is also one of eBay's problems, though, because of the sheer volume of items available at any one time. There are a couple of different ways to cut through all that and find stuff on eBay.

First, on the main eBay page (*www.ebay.com*), there is a Sports Memorabilia category. You can click on that and use the ensuing indexes to work your way through the list of items. This is probably the way to go if you are not looking for something in particular and just want to see what's available.

However, if you have a specific item you're looking for, you're usually best off it you search for if. Let's give that a try by searching for a World Series ring.

1. Go to the eBay home page at *www.eBay.com*.

2. Click on the Sport Memorabilia category link. You will go to the main Sports Memorabilia page, as you see in the following figure.

3. On the main Sports Memorabilia menu, type a search word or phrase ("World Series ring") in the Search field, click the Search only in Sports Memorabilia box, then click Search. This limits the search to the sports memorabilia category.

4. You will get a list of auction items. In some cases, you can even see a picture of the item being auctioned.

One Man's Opinion:

Auctions are a great way to find that hard-to-locate or offbeat item for your collection. Sometimes it's fun just to browse through an auction site and see the many different types of things that are available.

▼ **Try It Yourself**

▲

Enter your search criteria here.

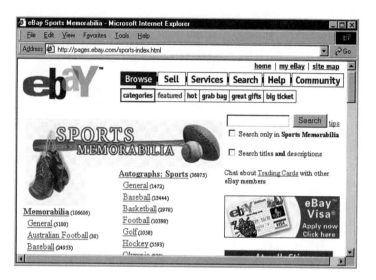

Rounding the Bases

This chapter covered the ins and outs of baseball memorabilia and collectibles on the Internet.

Among the topics covered were:

- How baseball card manufacturers help their customers with the hobby by offering information on the Web.

- Where you can go to help round out your baseball card collection.

- Where you can find game-used equipment or uniforms on the Web.

- How you can add other novelties, including bobble-head dolls, to your collection.

- How to use an auction Web site to help you find collectibles and memorabilia.

CHAPTER 16

Baseball in the Arts

There may be no sport that has had a bigger impact on the arts than baseball.

From *Bang the Drum Slowly* to *The Natural* to *Bull Durham*, baseball movies have been a successful part of mainstream moviegoing in America.

Baseball is also the most written-about sport in the country. There are more books—from novels to biographies—about baseball than any other sport. (In fact, here's one more!)

Baseball stories carry all the romance and drama of the real game and bring it to life.

But there's a lot more to "arts" than just movies and books. Baseball has also found its way into paintings, television, and so on.

We can't possibly cover it all here. But we'll take a look at some examples of baseball in the arts, and we'll walk through how to go about finding the art form for which you're looking.

You might just be surprised at what you find!

Finding Baseball Books on the Web

You often hear about people who have the dream of writing the great American novel. What a lot of people don't know is that it's already been written.

Philip Roth wrote *The Great American Novel,* and it's about baseball!

There are dozens of great baseball novels, and there's a plethora of outstanding nonfiction works about baseball as well. You can have a great time reading about your favorite sport, whether it's a story about a fictional team or the history of a real one.

What You'll Learn in This Chapter:

► Where you can find baseball books, both fiction and nonfiction.

► Where to go to find a copy of the baseball movie you've been wanting to add to your collection. We'll even show you where you can find highlight videos.

► Some examples of baseball artwork that you can discover online.

One Man's Opinion:
No baseball fan should go without reading *Why Time Begins on Opening Day* by Thomas Boswell. It's a great look at the role baseball plays in our society and why it is so treasured.

One Man's Opinion:

One of my favorite baseball novels is called *The Greatest Slump of All Time* by David Carkeet. It explores the inner workings of a baseball team, both on and off the field. It's both funny and poignant. Check it out!

There are, of course, some obvious ways to go about finding a particular baseball book on the Web. Most folks probably will start at either Amazon.com (*www.amazon.com*) or Barnes and Noble's Web site (*www.bn.com*).

Once you go to either one of those sites, you can do a search by author's name, book title, subject matter, and so on.

But what if you're interested in reading about baseball, but you don't have a firm idea of what you want to read? If you go to either one of those sites and do a search for the subject "Baseball," you're going to be so overwhelmed with matches that you won't be able to go through it all.

(You could, I suppose, go to your local bookstore or library and browse through the aisles, but this book is about the Internet, so let's focus on that option.)

Let's take a look at a couple of different ways to go about finding something that may interest you online.

Finding Baseball Books at Baseball Direct

If you're looking for good books about baseball, especially of the nonfiction variety, Baseball Direct is a good place to start.

A quick visit to the Baseball Direct Web site (*www.baseballdirect.com*) will show you why. Down the left side of the main page is an index, and one of the choices is Baseball Books. Click it and you will get a page that looks like the following figure.

Baseball Direct has divided its inventory into three topics:

- **Biographies**   You can find books on everyone from Babe Ruth to George Brett to Nolan Ryan to Orlando Cepeda in this area.

- **Team Histories**   Authorized histories of teams, unauthorized histories and even team encyclopedias are available here. Not every team is represented, but there's some great stuff here, including a book about the glory days of Charley Finley's Oakland A's in the 1970s.

- **Miscellaneous** Here's the catchall category, which features some great books including David Halberstam's *October 1964*. There's a lot of wonderful subject matter covered here.

Baseball Direct offers baseball books, especially nonfiction.

Movies and Videos, Too:

Baseball Direct is also a great source for movies and videos, too. They have a large selection in that area that's worth checking out.

They also offer CDs and instructional tapes and videos for baseball enthusiasts.

Baseball Direct doesn't have the largest selection of baseball books in the world, nor does it claim to. But it is a great place for the baseball fan to start when looking in general for a baseball title. If you want to get more specific and find a particular book, you'd be better off searching at one of the big booksellers.

Searching for Books

If there's a book out there that you've been looking for, then either Amazon.com or Barnes and Noble's Web site is the best place for you to start.

Lots of people like to read books by a particular author, too, and you can search that way as well. Or, you can browse through by subject matter. Let's look at how to do both.

Searching, as described earlier in this chapter, is pretty easy. Just plug in your search keywords into the search field and click Go or Search or whatever needs to be clicked. The results will appear on your screen, and generally, there will be a lot of them.

A Piece of Advice:
Narrow your search keywords as much as possible. A search for "baseball" will yield hundreds of results. A search for "hitting" will reveal fewer, and a search for "Ted Williams" will narrow it further. Be as specific as possible, and you'll get fewer matches, but they'll be more likely to match what you're actually looking for.

If a site offers it, narrow your search using a category. At Barnes and Noble's site, you can search by Author, Title, or Keyword.

For example, I went to Barnes and Noble's Web site (*www.bn.com*) and did a search for Frank Robinson, who won the Most Valuable Player award in both the National and American leagues, using Keyword. The result was a bunch of books written by someone named Frank Robinson, not books about the former outfielder for the Orioles and Reds.

Then, I went back and chose the category of Title and did the same search. My result this time was one book about the person I wanted, *the* Frank Robinson, as you can see in the following figure.

A search by title for Frank Robinson at bn.com yielded this result.

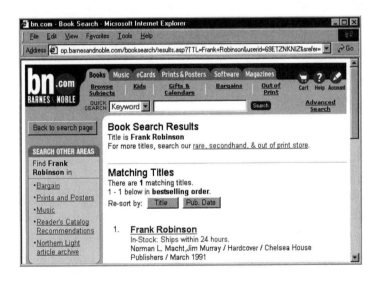

Now, let's browse by subject at Amazon.com.

Try It Yourself ▼

1. Go to the Amazon.com site at *www.amazon.com*. Click on the books tab, then click Browse Subjects.

2. Click the Sports & Outdoors category link, then click the Baseball link from the next page.

3. Within the Baseball category, click the subject you want. For this example, I chose General.

4. Then, you're into the lists of books. As you can see from the following figure, you see 25 books per page, but there are hundreds of titles waiting to be viewed (and purchased).

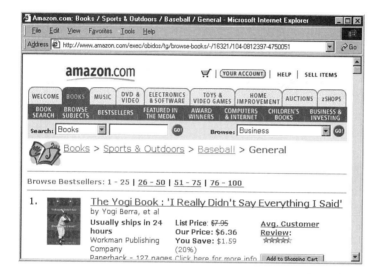

Amazon.com offers the ability to browse by subject.

There are, of course, plenty of other booksellers on the Internet. These are just a couple of examples; most of the other sites work in roughly the same way.

Finding Baseball Movies and Videos on the Web

Movies about baseball may not be as prevalent as books about the sport, but there are still many from which to choose. And whether your tastes are along the lines of *The Natural*, *Angels in the Outfield*, or *Major League*, those movies have been made into videos.

Now, you're probably not going to turn to the Internet to *rent* a movie for you and the missus to watch tonight, but the Web is a good place to go when you're looking for something to add to your collection permanently.

> **Movies from the Big Boys:**
>
> Many of the bigger e-tailers of books also offer videos for sale. For example, Baseball Direct offers instructional videos and videos authorized by Major League Baseball, like the official World Series video.
>
> You can buy movies from Amazon.com as well.
>
> And you'll probably find that most of the bigger Web sites we've covered throughout this book—everything from the Major League Baseball Web site to ESPN's to USA Today's—offer an area where they offer merchandise for sale. Many of those sites will include movies or videos about baseball.
>
> They are all good resources for you to use, and you should probably shop around a little before you make your decision.

If it's instructional videos you're looking for, one great place to shop is at *www.cybertown.net/sports/baseball/index.html.* You can see it in the following figure.

Instructional videos for players and coaches are available here.

These are great for players and coaches, and they are divided up by subject matter. So, you can quickly find resources for hitting, fielding, or whatever the case may be.

However, if what you want is a night at the movies, and it's a baseball movie you want to buy, you've got choices. You can pick one of the major movie e-tailers, or you can go to the source. And what better source than a place called Cooperstown Video? You can check out their selection at *www.cooperstown video.com/ movies.html* (see the following figure).

Cooperstown Video offers a complete selection of baseball movies.

> **Finding Baseball Artwork Online:**
>
> This category is a little harder to put your finger on online. There's such a broad range of what you might be looking for that it's difficult to track it down.
>
> Sad as it might be to say, your best starting point here might be to do a typical search at your favorite search engine.
>
> You might be surprised at what you find. For example, I did a search at Yahoo! for "baseball paintings" and got quite a few matches. One was a site that promotes artist Angela Fremont, who will create an oil painting of your baseball glove (*www.angelafremont.com*). It's an odd niche in the art world, but the paintings, based on their appearance on the Web, would make a great addition to a baseball fan's den (just a thought).
>
> I also came across a great collection of baseball portraits by artist Tom Rodrigues at *www.rodriguesstudio.com/artwork/baseball/index.shtml*. They are part of a series called Legends at the Stick, and they range from Jackie Robinson to Ty Cobb. A sampling can be seen in the following figure.

These paintings are part of a collection of baseball work by artist Tom Rodrigues.

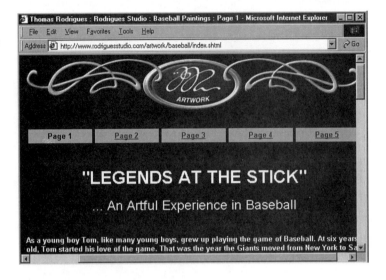

Rounding the Bases

"Art" is such a broad term that it's difficult to get your hands around it in the "real world," let alone in cyberspace.

But we tried in this chapter, and I think we did a pretty good job, if I do say so myself.

Here's what we covered:

- Baseball books—where to look for them, how to search for them, how to browse for them.

- Where to look for movies and videos on the Web, from instructional to historical to the big motion pictures that are now home videos.

- Some examples of artists' work on the Web about baseball.

CHAPTER 17

Planning Your Baseball Vacation Online

If you had to sit down and make a list of the top 10 places you want to visit before you die, what would make the list?

The Great Wall of China, or the Green Monster at Fenway Park? The ivy-covered buildings in London, or the ivy-covered walls of Wrigley Field? Buckingham Palace, or the House that Ruth Built?

Your answer may be all of the above. But since you're reading this book, then I'm guessing at least the baseball-related ones are on your list (unless you've already been to those places, of course).

There are other destinations that the baseball fan might want to take in before they pass from this Earth. Williamsport, Pennsylvania, home of the Little League World Series, might be one. Omaha, Nebraska, home of the College World Series, might be another. What about the Hall of Fame in Cooperstown, New York? Or some of the newer, retro ballparks like Camden Yards or Safeco Field?

They're all out there, waiting to be taken in. And some of them should be taken in as soon as possible, before they go the way of Tiger Stadium in Detroit.

What You'll Learn in This Chapter:

▶ Where to find the various ballpark tours that allow you to see many stadiums and many teams in one great trip.

▶ How to find trips to spring training destinations so you can see the players in a more up-close-and-personal way.

▶ Some museums or other historic places that you might want to take in on your vacation.

One Destination at a Time:

For many people, taking a baseball-specific vacation might not be feasible, for a variety of reasons.

But you can work a baseball stop into any trip, any time. For example, when I was a kid, we took a family vacation to the East Coast, and one of the places we hit along the way was the Baseball Hall of Fame.

If you're going to New York, why not plan it around a time when the Yankees are home? If you plan to do something like that, check out the major-league team's Web site for their schedule. On most of those sites, you can also buy tickets to the games, right there online.

These places can be visited as part of any vacation, be it a family trip or a "guys' weekend." But there are plenty of tour operators out there who offer special baseball packages that you might want to try. That's what this chapter is all about.

Ballpark Tours

One Man's Opinion:

Having grown up in Minnesota, my first baseball experience was at an erector-set ballpark, Metropolitan Stadium. But we Minnesotans came to appreciate the old "Met" after the Metrodome, perhaps the worst major-league park ever, opened in 1982.

So for me, the annual family trip to visit relatives in Texas always brings about a great retreat—a game at The Ballpark in Arlington.

There are many parks I'd like to visit before it's too late, but I'll always regret having missed seeing Tiger Stadium before it met the wrecking ball.

Imagine if you can a trip that takes you to eight different major-league stadiums in a 10-day period. It might sound a little bit exhausting, but consider that you might be able to take in eight different games involving a dozen or so different teams. In the process, you might be able to tick off four or five of the ballparks you've always wanted to visit.

Now, a person could certainly set up their own such trip. Heck, you don't even need to call your travel agent. You can hop behind the wheel of your car and, armed with a major-league schedule, hit a few picturesque stadiums and see some great baseball in the process.

However, just like it's easier to call a travel agent than to book your own trip to Disney World, it's easier to book such a baseball trip if you go through a company that sets these types of trips up.

Taking a Tour with Jay Buckley's Baseball Tours

Jay Buckley's Baseball Tours gives fans the opportunity to hit a large number of ballparks in a short period of time. They also offer shorter trips, including three-game series in a single city.

In 1999, for example, Jay Buckley Tours offered everything from a three-day stay in Milwaukee (for the last season at County Stadium) for an interleague series to an 11-day trip that included nine games and 17 teams at venues as special as Yankee Stadium, Comiskey Park, Tiger Stadium, Wrigley Field and Fenway Park.

The firm's Web site at *www.jaybuckley.com* gives the complete schedule for the upcoming season, including the availability of each trip. You can see the site in the following figure.

By the Way:

The tour operators listed here are just a few of many that offer baseball trips. We've tried to concentrate on those that specialize in baseball-only trips. There are many tour operators or travel agencies that offer trips that include a baseball component.

While touring all these major-league venues, you get a little taste of life in the minors by riding a bus around the country. In fact, some of the tours even include stops as minor-league ballparks, including Durham, North Carolina. You can even pick one that includes a stop at the "Field of Dreams" locale in Dyersville, Iowa. The tours begin in Wisconsin, and you have to find your own way there.

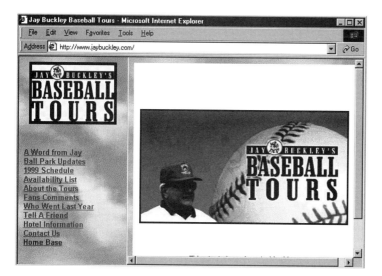

Jay Buckley's Baseball Tours offers a variety of different trips.

A Stroke of Luck:

In 1998, one of Jay Buckley's tours had a real stroke of luck. It just so happened that the tour swung through St. Louis on September 8, which just happened to be the night that Mark McGwire hit homer No. 62 to break Roger Maris' all-time major-league record.

They say that one of the wonders of baseball is that on any given night, you can see something truly magical.

And, it seems, on any given ballpark tour, you can see something historic as well.

Imagine booking a trip, say, in the spring, and getting lucky enough to see an event like that.

Pick Your Team, City, or Stadium with Sports Travel, Inc.

Options? You want options? I've got options for you.

Another sports-travel specialist on the Internet is Sports Travel, Inc. Every team in the majors is featured on at least one of its tours.

One of the nice features of this site is that you can target specific teams, stadiums, or geographical areas and hit exactly what you want to hit.

For example, if you really want to see Bank One Ballpark, home of the Arizona Diamondbacks, you can pick a tour that goes there. Or, if you really need to see the Tampa Bay Devil Rays, for example, you can pick a tour that will allow you to see them at least once. Or, if you don't care what teams you see but you want to go out to the East Coast, you can pick a trip based on that.

Let's take a trip through the Sports Travel Web site to find a trip that includes the Detroit Tigers, just as an example.

Try It Yourself ▼

1. Go to the Sports Travel, Inc. Web site at *www.4sportstravel.com/index.html.*

2. Click on the Baseball link on the left side of the Web page. This takes you to the baseball trips page.

By the Way:

This site also features the ability to arrange a "custom trip" if the scheduled offerings don't meet your needs. Just click on the Custom Travel link on the menu on the left side of the main baseball page.

3. On the baseball trips page, click on the picture of the suitcase (it says, "Click for 2000 trips" beneath it). This takes you to a search page you can use to find your trip, as you can see in the following figure.

4. On this page, you can search by location, team, stadium or month. If you just want to see the Tigers, you would choose them from the "Select by featured teams" window. If you really want to see them at their new park, Comerica Park, you would choose it from the stadiums list. Let's do that. Pick Comerica Park from the "Select by featured stadiums" list, then click Find My Trips.

5. You will see a list of five trips to choose from, including one that features 12 teams and six different stadiums.

▲

Use this page to search for your trip.

Planning a Trip to Spring Training

Lots of different tour operators offer trips designed around baseball's spring training. After all, spring training takes place in Florida and Arizona at a time of year when a lot of us northerners are looking for a southern destination and baseball is on our minds once again.

There is, however, at least one outlet that specializes in spring training tours designed around one of four different teams who hold spring training in Arizona.

If you're interested in sharing some warm springtime weather with the Oakland A's, San Francisco Giants, Seattle Mariners, or Colorado Rockies, this is the place for you: Spring Training Tours.

You can find their site at *www.springtrainingtours.com*. Click the Enter button when you get there, then click the Teams link. Pick the team you'd like to spend time with, and you'll get the information on their tour.

Other Options for Spring Fun:

There are a lot of different spring-training trips you can take and a lot of different places you can find them.

Many major-league teams offer spring training package on their individual Web sites. Just pick your team, go to their site, and look for spring training information.

Many tour operators who offer regular-season trips also offer spring excursions.

Finally, if you're planning a spring-break vacation, you can schedule in a spring training game or two as part of that trip!

By the Way:

Spring Training Tours' Web site indicates that it will offer some Florida destinations beginning in 2001.

A lot of amenities are included in the trip with the Oakland A's.

For example, the trip with the Oakland A's includes a lot of amenities. Along with airfare, lodging and other basics, it includes an autograph session with selected players, a season preview with Manager Art Howe, and more. Check it out in the following figure.

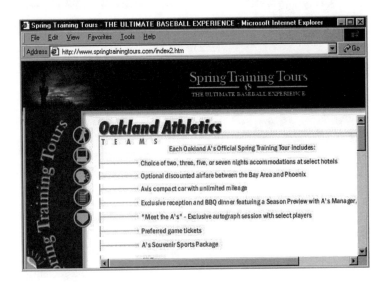

Hitting a Museum or Two

Whether you've been a baseball fan for a long time or are relatively new to the game, you can't help but enjoy a visit to a baseball museum.

It's a little (or big, in some cases) piece of history. It's a chance to learn about the great players of the past, and to better understand how they helped to shape the game into what it is today.

Of course, the be-all, end-all of museums is the National Baseball Hall of Fame and Museum in Cooperstown, New York.

Not only does it house the busts of all the great major-leaguers who have been enshrined there, but it is also home to numerous exhibits about the game's history.

Some of those exhibits are available online at the hall's Web site at *www.baseballhalloffame.org*. You can use the Web site to preview some of the many things you can see when you get to the museum.

Neyer's Nugget: I'd Rather Be a Fan

In some ways, being a baseball *fan* is better than being a baseball *player*. For one thing, we fans don't have to worry about those huge paychecks, which create more headaches than you'd think. And second, we fans generally enjoy the travel more than the players do.

Think about it. If you're a ballplayer, you fly into a new city and arrive at your hotel late in the evening. You sleep late the next day, get something to eat, and before you know it, it's off to the ballpark for batting practice and interviews. After the game, it's back to the hotel for a few drinks, and then the whole process begins anew. In other words, while ballplayers travel all over the country, they rarely have time for any serious sight-seeing.

But fans have the best of both worlds. Let's say that you're finally making a pilgrimage to Fenway Park, legendary home of the Red Sox. Well, the evening's game doesn't start until 7:05, which means you've got the whole day to enjoy the many pleasures of Boston. You can stroll along the Freedom Trail, tour the *USS Constitution*, or gawk at the beatniks in Harvard Square.

In my various baseball travels, I have also worked in visits to the Henry Ford Museum (Detroit), the Texas School Book Depository (Dallas), the Negro Leagues Baseball Museum (Kansas City), the Gateway Arch (St. Louis), the Empire State Building (New York, of course), the site of old Forbes Field (Pittsburgh), and the San Francisco waterfront (in addition to more second-hand bookstores than I can remember). And finally, there's my dream vacation, a vacation that would combine two of my great passions: baseball ("The National Pastime") and old Route 66 ("The Mother Road"). You start at Wrigley Field and end at Dodger Stadium, with a half-continent's worth of roadside attractions in between. I'll see you on the road!

One Man's Opinion:

Regardless of how great the Web is, and how great the Hall of Fame's Web site is, you can't beat a visit to the real thing. Use the Web site to whet your appetite for your actual visit.

You can see a piece of the Web site in the following figure.

*The Baseball Hall
of Fame's Web
site includes
online exhibits.*

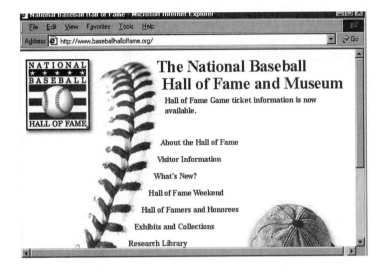

The Web site offers information about many of the real exhibits,
but there are some special "online exhibits" available on the site.
If you click on the Exhibits and Collections link, then click
Online Exhibits link, you'll see them. One features the members
of the 3,000-hit club, including Tris Speaker (see the following
figure).

*Tris Speaker is
featured as part
of the 3,000-hit
club online
exhibit.*

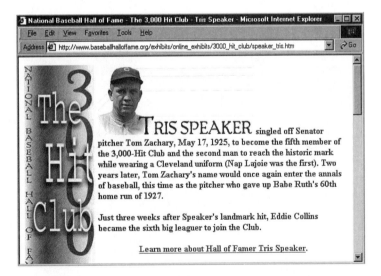

Here are a couple of other museums you may want to visit, either online or in person (or both):

- The Canadian Baseball Hall of Fame and Museum, located in St. Marys, Ontario, honors those who have contributed to baseball in Canada (although they don't have to be Canadian). The Web site is located at *www.baseballhof.ca*.

- The Babe Ruth Birthplace and Orioles Museum honors the Babe, who was born in Baltimore, and the Orioles. It is located near the Orioles new ballpark, Camden Yards. The Web site can be found at *www.baberuthmuseum.com*.

Rounding the Bases

Thousands of people take in a ballgame or visit a museum as part of a summer vacation. This chapter offered some advice to them, but focused more on those who want to make baseball the focus of a vacation, be it family or otherwise.

We covered:

- Where you can find information on ballpark tours offered by national tour companies.

- How you can choose a trip based on a region of the country, or a specific team or stadium that you want to see.

- Where to look to help you arrange a trip to a spring-training destination.

- Some museums that are located online, including the National Baseball Hall of Fame and Museum.

CHAPTER 18

Baseball on AOL

There are more than 20 million subscribers to America Online. That fact makes it the largest Internet service provider in the country. It also makes it a pretty good possibility that you are one of them.

If you're already a member of America Online, this chapter will help you find all the baseball information you want on the service. If you're not an AOL member and you're just reading this chapter because you're curious about what the service has to offer, chances are good that by the end of the chapter you'll want to join.

Lots of people who are not members of AOL don't understand what all the fuss is about. After all, they can get to all those same sites on the Internet that AOL members can, right?

That's true, but AOL has its own services that only its members can see (see "The Difference between AOL and the Internet"). It is those "Only on AOL" services that we will be covering in this chapter.

What You'll Learn in This Chapter:

▶ Where to find baseball news on America Online, including game coverage and team coverage.

▶ Where to find an up-to-the-minute scoreboard and league and team statistics.

▶ How to follow your favorite team on America Online, including joining a "Team Club."

▶ Where you can participate in chats and message boards on the service.

▶ What AOL has to offer to those who want to participate in a fantasy baseball league.

The Difference between AOL and the Internet:

Lots of people, even AOL members, don't understand the difference between AOL and the Internet.

To view the sites on the Internet, you need the services of an Internet Service Provider (ISP) to link your computer to the thousands of others that host those sites.

America Online is an ISP, true. You can use AOL to view all the same Internet sites that anyone else who is online can see.

However, AOL also offers its own services to members. These services are divided into 18 different topics, called "Channels" to which only members have access.

This also includes all of AOL's chat and message board areas. One of those Channels is called Sports, and includes AOL's coverage of the major leagues and other sports-related services.

After all, we've already covered the rest of the Internet in the rest of the book!

First, we'll look at the basics of baseball on AOL, such as how to get to the main baseball screen and where to find up-to-the-minute baseball coverage.

Then, we'll show you how to find the scores and statistics you want on AOL. We'll also look at AOL's chat and message boards for baseball fans, and at their fantasy baseball offerings.

AOL Sports Channel Basics

There's nothing that sports fans love more than a really good sports channel. That goes for television, of course, but it also goes for cyberspace.

America Online has a great Sports Channel for baseball fans (and fans of any other sport, for that matter). It's updated constantly, so that you can keep up with all the latest developments.

Like any good sports media outlet, you'll find previews of upcoming games, recaps of previous action, game stories, box scores, standings, statistics, etc. You'll also get live chat, message boards and all the little extras that make AOL a staple for many American households.

Before we get too deep into all the wonders of the Sports Channel (specifically baseball), you need to find it first. That part's pretty easy, but let's take a walk through it.

Try It Yourself ▼

1. When you log on to AOL, you are greeted by the Welcome screen (along with a few ads and some other windows, most likely). On the left side of the Welcome screen is the list of Channels.

2. Click the Sports button, and the main Sports Channel screen will appear, as you can see in the following figure.

3. To get to the main Baseball screen, also called the Baseball Forum, click Baseball from the Choose a Sport list of links.

▲ 4. The main Baseball screen appears, and you're there!

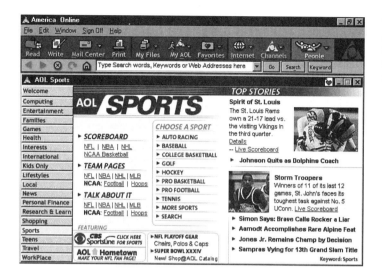

The main Sports Channel screen leads you to many of the Baseball offerings.

If you look at the main Sports Channel screen in the previous figure, you'll notice that it's divided into a number of different areas. Let's take a quick look at those areas:

- **Top Stories** On the right side of the screen, you'll get a brief summary of the top couple stories of the day, plus headlines for some other top stories. You can click on any of the links in that area to get more information on any of those stories.

- **Choose a Sport** In the center of the screen, this is where you click on Baseball to go to the main Baseball forum page.

- **Scoreboard** In season, click on the MLB link to go to the major league scoreboard page.

- **Team Pages** Click on the MLB link here and you'll go to a list of team pages from which you can choose.

- **Talk About It** Again, a click on the MLB link takes you to AOL's chat and message board area for baseball fans.

Here's the Scoop:
The Scoreboard, Team Pages and Talk About It areas are covered in more detail later in this chapter.

Baseball News, Scores, and Stats on AOL

Need a quick update on what's going on in the major leagues? The Baseball forum on AOL is the place to go.

Need to check the scores quick? AOL's Baseball Scoreboard is the place to go. Need to check in on the hitting leaders in the major leagues? AOL offers a statistics page that is the place to go.

In other words, no matter what you're looking for in terms of baseball information, AOL's got you covered, so to speak.

Baseball News

Few sports fans can get by on scores and statistics alone. We need to read about the flow of the game, or a preview of tonight's premier pitching match up, or an analysis or opinion column about the major leagues.

All of that and more is available from AOL. The main Baseball forum page contains all of it. To get there, just click Baseball from the Choose a Sport area on the main Sports Channel screen. Or, if you are a fan of AOL's keywords, use the keyword Baseball.

You'll go to the main Baseball forum page, as you can see in the following figure.

Read all the latest baseball news on the Baseball forum.

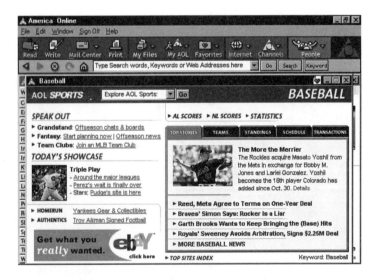

On the left side of the page are more areas of the Baseball forum you can go to, but the brunt of the baseball coverage will be found on the right side of the screen. There are five tabs there, and the Top Stories tab offers the biggest stories of the day. The last link in the Top Stories area is More Baseball News, which brings you more stories.

If there is a particular team that you are interested in reading about, click the Teams tab. You'll see a list of links to every team in the major leagues. Click on the team of your choice, and you'll go straight to that team's news page. An example can be seen in the following figure.

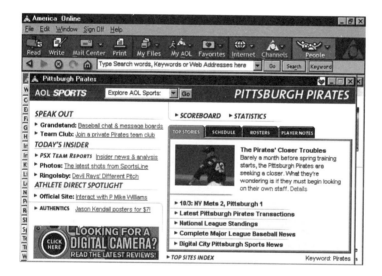

The Pittsburgh Pirates team page on AOL offers news about the Bucs.

Scores and Statistics

There are two ways to get to the main baseball scoreboard on AOL. First, you can click on the MLB link under Scoreboard in the Sports Channel's main screen. Or, you can click either AL Scores or NL Scores from the top of the Baseball forum's main page.

The statistics offerings are neatly organized and very thorough. To get there, just click the Statistics link at the top of the main Baseball forum page.

The statistics can be viewed in a number of ways. You can see the statistics page in the following figure.

Statistics are sortable by team, or by category.

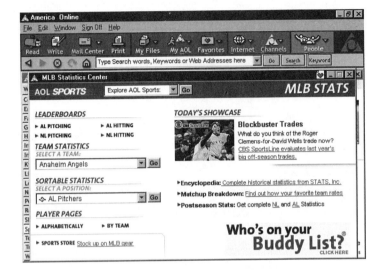

You can choose to view the statistics by team or by category. For example, you can view the batting or pitching leaders for the American League, National League, or both leagues combined.

If you came to see your favorite team's complete statistics, just select the team name from the list, and you'll get all the up-to-date information.

Want a Shortcut?

If you want to cut through all the steps and have a quick shortcut to the Baseball forum on AOL, I've got a little secret for you.

On the main Welcome screen, in the lower right-hand side, is an area called My Places. It's new to AOL 5, and it allows you to create a quick shortcut to a place you'll visit often.

To do it, click Set My Places. Pick the Sports menu, then click on Baseball, and it will be added to the My Places menu. Then, next time you want to go there, you just click the Baseball link in My Places, and you're there.

Another form of shortcut on AOL is through Favorite Places. Every AOL window or screen has a little heart icon in the upper-right corner. If a particular page (say, your favorite team's page on AOL) is one you want to visit often, go to that page and click the heart icon. Then click the Add to Favorites button, and you're done. Next time you want to go straight to that page, open the Favorites menu and click the link to it.

Talkin' Baseball on AOL

Back in Chapter 7, "Talkin' Baseball—The Hot Stove League," we covered newsgroups, chat and mailing lists. America Online offers all of that to its baseball-fan members.

To get started, you need to go to the Grandstand, which is home to all the talk about baseball on AOL. Just click on the link to the Grandstand from the main Baseball page. The Grandstand page is shown in the following figure.

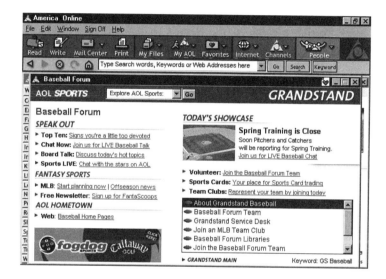

The Grandstand offers baseball chat and message boards.

Under the Speak Out header, you'll find four different ways to participate in chatter with other baseball fans on AOL:

- **Top Ten**   There's typically a Top-10 list, usually humorous, provided by CBS Sportsline. One recent day, the list was 10 ways John Rocker could fake sanity in order to pass his league-mandated psychological counseling.

- **Chat Now**   Live Baseball talk, 24 hours a day, 365 days a year, with other fans from around the country. Just click on the link to get started.

- **Board Talk**   Leads you to AOL's baseball message boards. There are numerous boards, including ones for the American League, National League, college, and minor-league baseball.

- **Sports LIVE**   Chat area that features guest chats with base-ball players, and other high-profile guests.

If, however, it's a mailing list you are looking for, check out one of AOL's Team Clubs. Just click on the Team Clubs link from the main Baseball page, and you'll get a list of Team Clubs you can join.

What they are, in fact, are mailing lists operated through America Online. Once you're a member (it just involves a few clicks), you'll receive special team reports, schedules, merchandise offers and more, all through your AOL email account.

Fantasy Leagues

You may remember that back in chapters 12-14, we covered play-ing in fantasy or rotisserie leagues, starting a league, or playing in a computer simulation baseball game.

AOL has all of those offerings and, in fact, they are offerings we have covered in those previous chapters. AOL has partnerships with CBS Sportsline's Commissioner.com, and with STATS, Inc.

Just use the keyword Fantasy Sports to get to the main fantasy window, which you can see in the following figure.

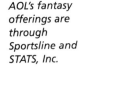

AOL's fantasy offerings are through Sportsline and STATS, Inc.

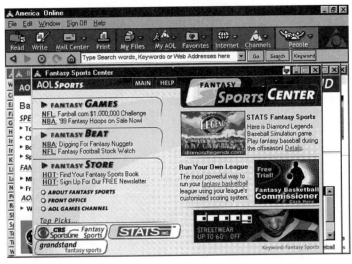

Commissioner.com, you may remember, offers leagues you can join or the ability for you to set up your own league and have the service act as the commissioner. STATS, Inc. also offers fantasy leagues but includes the Diamond Legends simulation game, allowing you to use players from the past to play in a league.

AOL also offers all the fantasy baseball advice and tips that are available through CBS Sportsline.

Rounding the Bases

America Online is an Internet Service Provider that offers its members an addition level of content that they can't get elsewhere.

Some of this content is provided through links to partners on the Internet, but much of it is AOL's only. Baseball fans will find a lot to like on AOL.

In this chapter, we covered the bases (so to speak) of AOL's baseball content. We covered:

- The basics of navigating the Sports Channel within AOL.

- Where you can find baseball news on AOL, and what that content typically is.

- How you can use your AOL membership to get the latest scores and statistics from the major leagues.

- How you can talk baseball on AOL through chat, message boards, and mailing lists called Team Clubs.

- Where you can find fantasy leagues and simulation games you can play through AOL and its partners.

CHAPTER 19

Over the Fence

Writing a book like this can make you a little goofy. You're researching Web sites, writing, writing some more, researching some more, and writing some more.

When you've reached this point, you're starting to lose control of your faculties. You start thinking that you might be crazy enough to own your own major-league team. You feel kind of like firing the manager, demanding a new stadium and signing a .240 lifetime hitter for $6 million a year.

I was worried that this type of lunacy might happen to me as my work on this book wound down to a final chapter. So, way back when we were working on the Table of Contents for this book, I put in a goofy chapter to help me out.

Here it is.

Perhaps more than any other sport, baseball lends itself to nuts. Nutty people, that is. It's probably all the "down" time that players spend at the ballpark—it allows time for the mind to wander.

You want proof that baseball can be goofy? How about Al Hrabosky, "the Mad Hungarian," standing behind the mound facing centerfield, then pounding the ball into his glove and turning to pitch to the next batter? How about first basemen playing tic-tac-toe with each other during the middle of a game? How about a midget being sent up to bat during a real game, for the sole purpose of drawing a walk? How about nicknames like "Spaceman" (Bill Lee) and "Psycho" Steve Lyons?

Need any more info?

This chapter is designed to look at the game a little differently. Baseball is fun to play and fun to watch, but lots of people have fun with the game in different ways.

What You'll Learn in This Chapter:

▶ The little "extra" pages that you can find on larger sites that are some of the jewels of the Internet.

▶ Some sites that look at baseball with a slightly more irreverent eye than you'll find elsewhere.

▶ Some baseball humor on the Internet.

Spend any time searching around the Internet (for any topic, not just baseball), and you'll find some off-beat material. This chapter is a collection of off-beat baseball material and sites that approach the game from a slightly different slant.

Covering the Game with a Cynic's Touch

Sometimes, it's fun to stop and take a look at the game of baseball in a different way.

People can get so wrapped up in coverage of the daily issues of games, transactions, standings and so on, that they forget to stop and have fun with it a little.

Your daily newspaper probably has a columnist who tends to look at sports with a more cynical eye. He might like to poke a little fun at the players, managers, even the owners of the teams and the leagues themselves.

Sometimes it can go too far, but on other occasions, it can be pretty darn funny.

There are columnists and others on the Web who offer an irreverent look at the majors, and there are also entire Web sites that look at the game slightly off-kilter.

Following the Game with Strikethree.com

Back in Chapter 4, "Following the Major Leagues Online," we covered some sites that offer up-to-the-minute information for baseball fans. They're great sites, and a great way to keep up with the latest news from around the major leagues.

If you want to have a little laugh at the same time, you might just want to check out Strikethree.com (*www.strikethree.com*).

Strikethree.com offers news from respected news sources, but adds an irreverent touch to it that will give fans a chuckle as they read. You can keep up with the scores through a live scoreboard, you can follow the news with updates from around the league.

But Strikethree.com offers some other features that make it truly unique. There are analysis pieces and columns written by staff writers, all of whom have an uncanny ability to elicit a laugh.

Even the headlines are humorous. For example, when the Orioles signed Aaron Sele in January of 2000, most sites carried a headline like, "Sele leaves Rangers for Orioles," or words to that effect. Strikethree.com's headline read, "(Orioles owner Peter) Angelos finds change in sofa, signs Sele." You can check out the main page in the following figure.

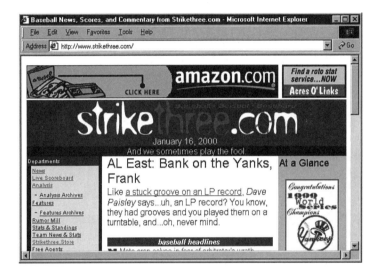

Strikethree.com offers an irreverent look at baseball.

There's lots of great information here and, while you might find a few errors in grammar and spelling, few baseball fans would care when they read the material.

How Do You Want to Vote?

Strikethree.com likes to poke fun at certain team owners, particularly those who have huge money and not a lot of ability to control it.

Frequent targets appear to be those owners who don't have a baseball background, but just got into the sport because they're loaded.

Certain teams also get hit hard on the site, including the Los Angeles Dodgers. A recent "Insta-Poll" on the site offered this question:

"What will the Dodgers do with the salary they recently freed up?"

The possible answers: "Franklin Mint Giveaway Night; Armani uniforms; Fund program to clone Mark Grudzielanek; Hire Jim Carrey for *Star Wars: Episode II*; Get a GM who doesn't suck."

The last choice was leading the poll at this writing.

The news briefs you can find on the News link are particularly funny. They appear to be normal news stories until the last line or so. For example, on the story about Baltimore's signing of Sele, it closed, "Sele is allowing the Orioles to defer $2M of each year's salary, which apparently will go toward the 'Feed Albert Belle' fund…"

The Bucketfoot Baseball Newsletter

The Internet is a lot like the power alleys at Coors Field: vast. You can find all sorts of baseball newsletters and opinion pieces out there, but one of the best is the Bucketfoot Baseball Newsletter.

The newsletter's Web site at *www.bucketfoot.com* says the product "is an informal publication by two guys who run up huge phone bills talking baseball."

You can find past issues of the newsletter on the site, which you can see in the following figure.

The Bucketfoot Baseball Newsletter offers a different angle on the game.

Among the articles is a plea for a West Coast version of the National Baseball Hall of Fame, and a theory on the "lively"

baseball (the Haitians who make the ball switched from decaf to a dark French roast, so the balls are more tightly wound).

It's great for a laugh.

The Hidden Jewels of the Internet

We're on the final chapter of this book, and we've done a lot of surfing together. You've followed the directions here to find numerous sites on the Web. While doing this, you've probably had something catch your eye, and it has led you off on an Internet tangent.

That's just fine. In fact, some of the best things you can find on the Web are found through exactly that method.

In the course of preparing for this book, I came across a number of different pages on the Web that either made me laugh or were offbeat and interesting in the type of material they presented.

If you don't mind, indulge me a little here and take a look at the few of them.

Casey Stengel's 1958 Senate Testimony

In 1958, Casey Stengel testified in the Senate Anti-Trust and Monopoly subcommittee hearings. Stengel was a great manager, but his ability to put words together made Yogi Berra sound like Ben Franklin.

Once you've gone through Stengel's testimony, you will wonder what those Senators said to their spouses when they got home that night. Perhaps it was Casey's duty to confuse the subcommittee so much that they would let Major League Baseball do whatever it wanted to do.

I came across Stengel's testimony in two different formats. You can read the complete testimony at *www.fastball.com/foulpole/casey/casey1.html* (see the following figure).

Or, you can hear excerpts of the actual testimony at *earthstation1.com/stengel.html*.

By the way:
You will probably have to download a freeware program called True Speech Player in order to hear Stengel's testimony on this site.

Casey Stengel's testimony is worth a read.

Just One Excerpt to Whet Your Whistle:

Casey Stengel was a man of many words, and not many of them made any sense. At one point in his testimony, Stengel is asked why, in his opinion, Major League Baseball wants the bill passed. He gives a long answer that has nothing to do with the question, so the question is asked again.

Stengel responds, "I would say I would not know, but would say the reason why they would want it passed is to keep baseball going as the highest paid ball sport that has gone into baseball and from the baseball angle, I am not going to speak of any other sport. I am not here to argue about other sports, I am in the baseball business. It has been run cleaner than any business that was ever put out in the 100 years at the present time. I am not speaking about television or I am not speaking about income that comes into the ballparks: You have to take that off. I don't know too much about it. I say the ballplayers have a better advancement at the present time."

Okay...

Remembering Harry

Baseball fans may have a love affair with their favorite players, but they often have similar feelings about the broadcasters who have brought the games into their homes over the years.

Harry Caray was one of the most beloved and imitated broadcasters in the history of the game. He broadcast games on both radio and television, and built a national following doing the Cubs games on nationwide cable on WGN. His rendition of "Take Me

Out to the Ballgame" during the seventh inning stretch at Cubs home games is the stuff of legend.

There are Harry tributes all over the Web, many of them from fans of the late broadcaster. But I'll direct you to a page of audio clips brought to you by the Cubs themselves. You can find the page at *www.cubs.com/caray-audio.htm*.

Some of the clips are directly from game action, while others are from other events, such as his induction into the Baseball Hall of Fame. It's worth a listen.

By the Way:
If you don't have the Real Audio Player, you'll need to download it in order to listen to these clips.

Chris Berman's Nicknames

Whether you are a fan of Bert "Be Home" Blyleven or Al "Cigarette" Leiter, you are probably a fan of Chris Berman.

Berman is one of the original ESPN anchors who has gained fame from both his skill in the business and the humorous nicknames he tags players with.

Part of what has made ESPN a success as a network is the fact that they don't take themselves too seriously. Berman is the king of not taking oneself too seriously.

There are a number of archives of the nicknames Berman has used, but one of the most thorough can be found at *www.op.net/~lmk/baseball/berman.htm*. You can see it in the following figure.

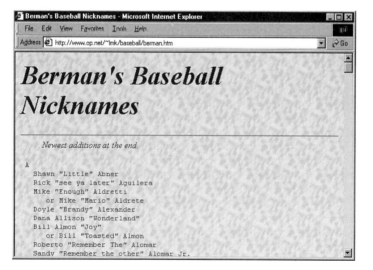

Chris Berman's nicknames are compiled here.

360-Degree Views

A number of major-league teams offer views of their stadium from different locations around the park. The Colorado Rockies go a little bit further, offering a 360-degree view of Coors Field (*www.coloradorockies.com/coorsfield/media/field.html*).

It's a neat little feature, giving you the opportunity to get the "Coors Field Experience" regardless of where you might be located.

Get the "Coors Field Experience" with a 360-degree view of the stadium.

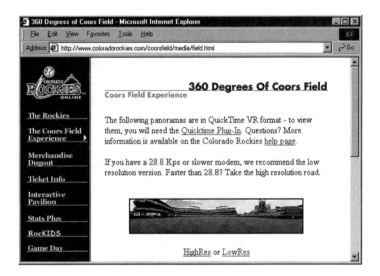

Baseball Heckle Depot

The Baseball Heckle Depot is the home for all those bench-jockeys out there who love to sit in the dugout, riding the opponent into the ground.

About 500 different "heckles" can be found on the site, including such zingers as "I've seen better swings on the playground," to "You couldn't hit sand if you fell off a camel."

The site (*www.heckledepot.com*) can be seen in the following figure.

The heckles are broken down by target, that is, if you want to learn a few ways to criticize an umpire, click on the Umpire link and you'll see the list.

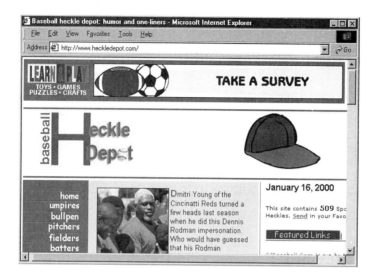

The Baseball Heckle Depot offers ideas to bench jockeys.

Rounding the Bases

In this chapter, we covered some of the more offbeat Web sites and pages that you can find on the Internet. If you like to look at baseball a little cockeyed, then this was the chapter for you.

Among the items we covered:

- Some sites that offer news, scores, and so on for the major leagues, but do so in a slightly more offbeat manner than is usually the case.

- Some pages that can be considered hidden jewels on the Web—they offer great material but aren't the focus of their own site.

- A number of sites that feature humorous material such as special sound or video clips.

PART VI

Appendixes

APPENDIX A

Recommended Baseball Web Sites

In this appendix, you will find loads of URLs, listed by the chapter to which the sites are relevant. Remember that the Web is constantly changing—and rapidly so.

Chapter 1: Learning the Rules Online

www.majorleaguebaseball.com	The major leagues' official Web site
www.legion.org/BASEBALL/home.htm	The Web site for American Legion baseball
www.littleleague.org	Little League Baseball's official Web page
www.upll.org	The Union Park of Orlando, Florida, Little League Web site
www.abua.com	The Amateur Baseball Umpires Association Web site
www.umpire.org	An offshoot of the ABUA site, this address offers many resources for umpires, including links to umpire sites at the NCAA and major-league levels
www.majorleagueumps.com	The association for major-league umpires Web site

Chapter 2: Coaching and Equipment

www.pitching.com	Former Boston Red Sox pitcher Dick Mills' pitching site
www.wk20.com	The Web site of Wendell Kim, third-base coach for the Boston Red Sox

www.eteamz.com/baseball/instruction/	The baseball instruction area of eteamz, a top-notch Internet site for coaches
www.chre.vt.edu/f-s/rstratto/CYS/	Virginia Tech University's newsletter, published to help coaches of all sports be better prepared
www.hscoaches.org	The National High School Athletic Coaches Association site
members.accessus.net/~icacoach/	The Illinois Coaches Association site
www.jbssinc.com	The Fisher Web site offers information on a valuable part of baseball—the sunflower seed
www.baseballdepot.com	For information on just about anything needed for baseball, try the Baseball Depot's site
www.123-baseball.com	Site of equipment retailer 123 Baseball
www.ziptrainer.com	The Zip Baseball Trainer site claims to improve players' throwing mechanics
www.americanmold.com/accubat/	The Accubat aids coaches in hitting consistent grounders and popups

Chapter 3: Development of the Game

www.majorleaguebaseball.com	The major leagues' official Web site
www.totalbaseball.com	Total Baseball Online provides the best encyclopedia-style look at the history of the game
www.baseball-almanac.com	Baseball Almanac offers a more off-beat history of the major leagues
www.negroleaguebaseball.com	Offers a historical look at the Negro Leagues and their players
www.blackbaseball.com	BlackBaseball's site offers historical information on the Negro Leagues, the teams and their players

members.aol.com/legendlady/	Offers a history of the All-American Girls Professional Baseball League and links to upcoming events
www.exploratorium.edu/baseball/ girlsofsummer.html	Highlights women's impact on baseball throughout history
www.assumption.edu/HTML/Academic/ history/Hi113net /AAGPBL%20Charm% 20School%20Guide/	The actual guide for appearance and manners the women of the American Girls Professional Baseball League had to follow

Chapter 4: Following the Major Leagues Online

www.majorleaguebaseball.com	The major leagues' official Web site
www.totalbaseball.com	Provides the best encyclopedia-style look at the history of baseball
espn.go.com/mlb/index.html	ESPN's main baseball home page
cbs.sportsline.com/mlb/index.html	CBS Sportsline's baseball server
www.usatoday.com/sports/mlb.htm	USA Today's main baseball page offers baseball news in bite-size pieces
www.usatoday.com/bbwfront.htm	Shares content of the magazine Baseball Weekly
www.sportsline.com	CBS television offers CBS Sportsline, a great sports Web site
www.sportingnews.com/ baseball/scoreboard/	A scoreboard is offered at the Sporting News' Web site
espn.go.com/today/sco.html	Access schedules at ESPN's baseball site
www.sportsline.com/u/baseball/mlb/ sched.htm	CBS Sportsline's schedule page
espn.go.com/tvlistings/index.html	If you want to watch a game on TV, check out ESPN's TV listings

Chapter 5: Finding Your Favorite Team or Player Online

www.majorleaguebaseball.com	The Major League Baseball site
www.angelsbaseball.com	The official site for the Anaheim Angels
www.azdiamondbacks.com	The official site for the Arizona Diamondbacks
www.atlantabraves.com	The official site of the Atlanta Braves
www.theorioles.com	The official site for the Baltimore Orioles
www.redsox.com	The official site of the Boston Red Sox
www.cubs.com	The Chicago Cubs' official Web site
www.chisox.com	The official site of the Chicago White Sox
www.cincinnatireds.com	The official site of the Cincinnati Reds
www.indians.com	The official site of the Cleveland Indians
www.coloradorockies.com	The Colorado Rockies' official Web site
www.detroittigers.com	The official site of the Detroit Tigers
www.flamarlins.com	The Florida Marlins' official Web site
www.astros.com	The Houston Astros' official Web site
www.kcroyals.com	The official Web site of the Kansas City Royals
www.dodgers.com	The Los Angeles Dodgers' official site
www.milwaukeebrewers.com	The official site of the Milwaukee Brewers
www.mntwins.com	The official site for the Minnesota Twins
www.montrealexpos.com	The official Web site of the Montreal Expos
www.mets.com	The New York Mets' official Web site

www.yankees.com	The official Web site for the New York Yankees
www.oaklandathletics.com	The Oakland Athletics' official site
www.phillies.com	The official site of the Philadelphia Phillies
www.pirateball.com	The Pittsburgh Pirates' official Web site
www.padres.com	The San Diego Padres' official site
www.sfgiants.com	The official Web site of the San Francisco Giants
www.mariners.org	The official site for the Seattle Mariners
www.stlcardinals.com	The official Web site of the St. Louis Cardinals
www.devilrays.com	The Tampa Bay Devil Rays' official Web site
www.texasrangers.com	The official site for the Texas Rangers
www.bluejays.ca	The Toronto Blue Jays' official Web site
espn.go.com/mlb/clubhouses/index.html	ESPN's team index
www.sportsline.com	CBS Sportsline
www.thesportingnews.com	The Sporting News
www.totalbaseball.com	Total Baseball offers baseball team pages
foxsports.com	The Fox Sport Web site shares baseball information
examiner.com/sports/	Sports coverage from the San Francisco Examiner newspaper
www.wcco.com/sports/twins/	The Minnesota Twins' home page on a local television/radio station's Web site
www.yahoo.com	The Yahoo search engine
www.geocities.com/Colosseum/Track/7004/	Forum gives fans a chance to sound off
www.2131.com	Cal Ripken, Jr.'s official Web site offers day-to-day coverage as well as details of his off-field activities

Chapter 6: Stats, Stats, and More Stats

www.majorleaguebaseball.com	Major League Baseball's Web site
espn.go.com	ESPN's Web site
espn.go.com/mlb/statistics/index.html	The baseball statistics page on ESPN's Web site
statsc.freeservers.com/mlb_index.html	Historical team and player stats for the last three decades are found on the Major League Baseball statistics page
www.highboskage.com	Predicts the ability of a player to impact his team's runs scored and/or runs allowed total
www.baseballstuff.com	Baseball Stuff site
www.baseballstuff.com/btf/pages/essays/jameserp.htm	An essay on the Estimated Runs Produced statistic
riot.ieor.Berkeley.edu/~baseball/	Minds at the University of California-Berkeley came up with an "improved" way to determine what a team must do to make the playoffs
www.sabr.org	The Society for American Baseball Research is comprised of baseball lovers who combine history and statistics to study the game
www.stathead.com	Claims to be the Internet's most complete free baseball research library
www.thinkingbaseball.com	Offers articles, daily updates and trade analyses

Chapter 7: Talkin' Baseball—The Hot Stove League

www.mlbfan.com	Web site with chat rooms for baseball fans
www.4-lane.com/sportschat/newsc/bb_index.html	Baseball Chat! is a good site for baseball fans to "talk" with others
www.baseballboards.com	Web site devoted to baseball bulletin boards
www.baseballstuff.com/guide/index.html	Lists links to USENET Newsgroups

www.enteract.com/~bc/bblistservs.html	Offers complete list of baseball-related mailing lists

Chapter 8: Minor League Baseball Online

espn.go.com/minorlbb/	ESPN's main minor-league home page
www.baseballamerica.com	Baseball America does great job of putting perspective on minor leagues
www.minorleaguebaseball.com	The official site for Minor League Baseball
www.ilbaseball.com	A complete resource for followers the Class AAA International League
www.northernleague.com	Site of the Northern League, a 16-team league stretching from the Dakotas to the Eastern seaboard
www.majorleaguebaseball.com/u/ baseball/mlbcom/1999/aft/	Offers coverage and feature stories on the Arizona Fall League
www.squeezebunt.com/azfall.html	Covers baseball in Arizona

Chapter 9: College Baseball Online

chili.collegesportsnews.com/ baseball/default.htm	The College Sports News covers college baseball well
www.FANSonly.com/channels/ news/sports/m-basebl/	FANSonly offers breaking news about college baseball as well as individual team pages
www.ncaa.org/stats/baseball.cgi	Stats site for the NCAA
www.big12sports.com	The main Big 12 Conference Web page
www.big12sports.com/bbo/ bbc/index.html	The Big 12 Conference's baseball pages
www.sec.org/teams/base/	The Southeastern Conference baseball Web site highlights some of the country's top teams
www.hurricanesports.com	Main sports page of the Miami Hurricanes
mgoblue.com/baseball/	Web site for the Michigan Wolverines' baseball team

www.ncaabaseball.com	The official College World Series Web site
www.ncaachampionships.com/sports/base/	Covers national championships at all levels of college baseball

Chapter 10: A mateur Baseball Online

www.legion.org/baseball/home.htm	The American Legion base-ball Web site has informa-tion for organizers, coaches, and fans
www.baberuthleague.org	The Babe Ruth League Web site includes everything from history to upcoming camps
lmontco.freeservers.com	Information for current and prospective players for the Lower Montco American Legion is found at its Web site
www.hsbaseballweb.com	The High School Baseball Web site is for anyone interested in high school baseball
www.pony.org	A good resource for players and other interested in the PONY league
www.littleleague.org	The Little League Web site
www.aaubaseball.org	A Web site specifically for baseball put together by the Amateur Athletic Union
www.cbweb.com	A tournament clearing house for teams at all levels

Chapter 11: International Baseball Online

www.inter.co.jp/baseball/	The English-language site for Japanese professional baseball
www.hawkstown.com	Most of the Fukuoka Daiei Hawks' site is in Japanese
www.nbcolympics.com	NBC's Olympic site is packed with information on every sport, including baseball
www.olympics.com/eng/sports/BB/about/	The baseball page at the official Olympics site

www.olympics.com/engl	The English-language home page for the Olympic Games
www.baseball.ch	A good resource for people interested in the World Cup and Intercontinental Cup, sponsored by the International Baseball Association
www.usabaseball.com	Includes information on all USA Baseball teams
www.bbf.org	Follows British national teams
www.baseball.ca	Shares information on baseball in Canada

Chapter 12: Playing in an Online Fantasy League

espn.go.com	Main ESPN Web site, offering fantasy leagues in a wide variety of sports
www.baseballmanager.com	A fantasy-style baseball game for Internet users
fantasybaseball.commissioner.com	Offers four ways to play fantasy baseball
baseball.smallworld.com	Small World Baseball combines traditional fantasy baseball with a stock market-like factor
www.usatoday.com/sports/baseball/ rotisix.com	USA Today's Rotisserie Corner is full of resources for fantasy players
www.rotonews.com/baseball/	Gives complete player rankings at every position and predictions for the upcoming season
www.rotojunkie.com	A less-than-objective site for rotisserie information

Chapter 13: Starting Your Own League Online

espn.go.com	ESPN's Web site
commissioner.com	Site for an e-commissioner
baseball.commissioner.com	Offers e-commissioners for baseball fantasy leagues

www.spinstats.com	Spin Stats is one of many statistics services found on the Internet
fm220.Colorado.edu/~coyle/ Baseball.html	Site for the Boulder Valley League Baseball fantasy league

Chapter 14: Computer Baseball Games

www.strat-o-matic.com	Offers online ordering, fixes, patches, and tech support for Strat-O-Matic computer games
www.geocities.com/Colosseum/3211/	The Twentieth Century Baseball Association Web site
www.nasbl.com	The North American Strat-O-Matic Baseball League covers the league like the big media outlets
www.diamond-mind.com	Allows you to play baseball live over the Internet
www.stats.com	Web site for Stats, Inc., which offers the Diamond Legends game

Chapter 15: Collectibles and Memorabilia Online

www.topps.com	The Topps baseball card manufacter's site
www.wwriches.com/ap/	This site offers baseball cards for sale
www.memory.loc.gov/ammem/ bbhtml/bbhome.html	Library of Congress' online archive of baseball cards from 1887-1914
www.greyflannel.com	Sells game-worn uniforms from professional players
www.boombats.com	Sells bats that once belonged to professional players
www.shoppressbox.com	Novelties and other collectibles can be found at this e-tailer
www.shoppressbox.com/pressbox/ mlb.com	The Press Box offers a Major League Baseball page
www.bobblehead.com	Sells the "traditional" bobble-head dolls

www.sportbobbers.com	Offers bobbers of current and former baseball greats
www.bobbing.com	Offers bobbing head dolls and figurines of players in several sports
auctions.sportingnews.com	Auctions of sports memorabilia are found on the Sporting News' Web site
www.ebay.com	Online auction service offers sports memorabilia

Chapter 16: Baseball in the Arts

www.amazon.com	Web site for Amazon.com, which offers books and videos on baseball
www.bn.com	Bookstore Barnes and Noble's Web site
www.baseballdirect.com	Offers baseball books, movies, videos, CDs, and instructional tapes for baseball fans
www.cybertown.net/sports/baseball/index.html	Instructional videos for players and coaches can be found here
www.cooperstownvideo.com/movies.html	Offers a complete selection of baseball movies
www.angelafremont.com	Promotes an artist who will create an oil painting of your baseball glove
www.rodriguesstudio.com/artwork/baseball/index.shtml	Offers baseball portraits done by artist Tom Rodrigues

Chapter 17: Planning Your Baseball Vacation Online

www.jaybuckley.com	Travel agency that offers baseball tours
www.4sportstravel.com/index.html	Sports Travel, Inc. offers a variety of tours
www.springtrainingtours.com	Outlet that specializes in spring training tours in Arizona
www.baseballhalloffame.org	Web site for the National Baseball Hall of Fame and Museum in Cooperstown

www.baseballhof.ca	Canadian Baseball Hall of Fame and Museum honors those who contributed to baseball in Canada
www.baberuthmuseum.com	Honors Baltimore born Babe Ruth and the Orioles

Chapter 18: Baseball on AOL

There were no Web sites listed in this chapter.

Chapter 19: Over the Fence

Strikethree.com	Offers news with an irreverent touch
www.bucketfoot.com	Bucketfoot Baseball Newsletter shares a different view of baseball
www.fastball.com/foulpole/casey/casey1.html	Casey Stengel's testimony in the Senate Anti-Trust and Monopoly subcommittee hearings
earthstation1.com/stengel.html	Hear excerpts of Casey Stengel's Senate subcommittee testimony at this site
www.cubs.com/caray-audio.htm	An audio tribute to Harry Caray offered by the Chicago Cubs
www.op.net/~lmk/baseball/berman.htm	Compilation of nicknames created by ESPN anchor Chris Berman
www.coloradorockies.com/coorsfield/media/field.html	Sports a 360-degree view of Coors Field, home of the Colorado Rockies
www.heckledepot.com	Offers ideas to bench jockeys who like to deliver zingers

APPENDIX B

Glossary

A

AAU—The Amateur Athletic Union (AAU) sponsors national competitions in a variety of sports, including baseball. AAU teams can be local teams that are part of another organization, such as Legion or Babe Ruth teams, or they can be separate teams put together on a regional level to compete in AAU events.

Accubat—A cross between a fungo bat and a racquetball racquet. It allow coaches to hit consistent grounders and popups to players in order to save time otherwise spent chasing mis-hits.

All-American Girls Professional Baseball League—A professional baseball league composed of women. It existed for a short time during World War II.

American Legion baseball—Sponsored by local American Legion posts, these baseball teams are comprised of players ages 15–18. It is the largest baseball program for high-school age youths.

America Online—The largest Internet service provider in the United States.

Arizona Fall League—A league set up the majors in order to offer players a greater chance to develop in the offseason while maintaining contact with their major-league organizations.

B

Babe Ruth League—The league was formed in the 1950s in Trenton, New Jersey, and quickly became a national organization. Played at the high school level, it also offers a division for 13–15 year olds. The league also has grown to include three levels of girls' softball.

batting average—A baseball player's ratio of base hits to times at bat, as a rate per thousand.

Big 12 Conference—It includes some of the perennial powers in college baseball, including Texas A&M, Baylor, Oklahoma State, and others.

boxscore—Found in the newspaper, it's the printed score of a baseball game. It gives the names and positions of the players and a record of the game arranged in tabular form.

bulletin board—Like a cork bulletin board, bulletin boards on the Internet allow users to "tack up" a message where it stays for other people to reach whenever they so desire.

bullpen—The area where pitchers warm up before they're brought into a game.

C

catcher's interference—When the catcher inhibits the batter's swing in some way.

chat room—Places on the Internet where people can send messages to each other ("chat") about their favorite topics, such as baseball.

closer—A pitcher who is brought in at the end of the game to seal the win for his team.

College World Series—Held annually in Omaha, Nebraska, this event includes the top eight college teams in the nation. After qualifying in regionals, the teams play off in a double-elimination format that is one of the best showcases of college athletics.

commissioner—The person who coordinates the functions of a league—a fantasy baseball league, for example.

E

earned run average (ERA)—The average number of earned runs per nine innings scored against a pitcher. It's found by dividing the total of earned runs scored against him by the total number of innings pitched and multiplying by nine. An earned run is a run that scores without benefit of an error before the fielding team has a chance to make the third out of the inning.

email—Electronic mail.

error—A defensive mistake in baseball, other than a wild pitch or walk, that under normal play would have resulted in an out or the prevention of the advancement of a base runner.

ESPN—The Entertainment and Sports Programming Network.

F

FANSonly—An organization that offers online management to collegiate athletic departments for their Web sites.

fantasy baseball—Fantasy baseball lets you be the manager of a major-league team. Leagues are generally made up of eight to 12 teams. Each person in the league owns a "franchise" made up of real major-league players "drafted" before the start of the season. The league is led by a "commissioner," who is responsible for upholding the league's rules and keeping track of the rosters. Franchise owners set their starting lineups and those players' statistics count toward league results.

farm team—A minor-league baseball team associated with a major-league team. The farm team serves as a training ground for future major leaguers.

franchise—Another name for a baseball team.

fungo bats—A bat designed to hit fly balls. It's used to give baseball players practice in fielding.

G

Gold Glove—An award given to major leaguers who demonstrate exceptional fielding skills.

I

infield fly rule—It protects baserunners in the event of a pop fly in the infield. When the batter hits a pop fly in the infield, the batter is automatically out. Runners can still advance after a catch, but don't have to.

International Baseball Association—This organization sponsors international competitions such as the World Cup and Intercontinental Cup.

Internet Service Provider—Links your computer to the thousands of others who host Internet sites.

L

leadoff hitter—The team's first person to bat in an inning.

list draft—In simulated baseball leagues that use list drafts, owners rank their players by position and a computer determines who they get.

Little League Baseball—For children ages 12 and younger, this organization crowns a national champion in several age divisions each year. It holds a World Series annually in Williamsport, Pennsylvania, in which children from around the world have the opportunity to play for the title.

live draft—In simulated baseball leagues that use live drafts, players are chosen in real time through a means similar to a chat room. You pick your player and it appears on the screen for all the other owners to see.

M

magic number—The number of games the leading team must win or its nearest competitor must lose in order for the team to clinch a division title or playoff berth.

mailing list—These are like bulletin boards in that when you send a message to the list, everyone else sees it. The key difference is they have to see it because it comes to them as an email.

Major League Baseball—The highest classification in professional baseball in the United States and Canada.

memorabilia—Mementos or keepsakes worthy of remembrance. Baseball memorabilia can include everything from baseball cards to a jersey or bat used by a major leaguer.

Minor league baseball—A league below the major leagues that still involves professional players.

moderated—Some Internet bulletin boards are moderated, meaning a person is in charge of watching over the site to make sure conversation doesn't get out of control.

N

National Association of Professional Baseball Leagues—This organization oversees all of minor-league baseball.

National Baseball Hall of Fame and Museum—Found in Cooperstown, New York, this museum is home to a multitude of exhibits about the history of baseball.

NCAA—The National Collegiate Athletic Association.

Negro Leagues—Before Jackie Robinson broke the color barrier, only whites were allowed to play Major League Baseball. Because of this, African Americans played in their own league from the early 1900s until the 1940s.

newsgroups—They are like bulletin boards, but you have to "subscribe" to them in order to read the messages.

Northern League—A 16-team minor-league baseball conference that stretches from the Dakotas to the Eastern seaboard.

P

pennant—A professional baseball championship.

PONY League Baseball—Protect Our Nation's Youth (PONY) includes more than 500,000 children today. The program started with children ages 13–15, but now offers programs to boys and girls (softball) ages 5–18.

private league—A fantasy baseball league that allows you to determine who can play with you.

prospect—A player the team hopes will become an integral part of the organization in the future.

public league—Fantasy baseball leagues in which you are matched against other players from around the world. You often are dropped in a league with people you've never met before.

R

record—The number of games a team has won or lost.

RBI—Run batted in.

rotisserie league—It's a game in which anyone can manage their own major-league team. Hitters and pitchers accumulate stats over a period of time in certain statistical categories. All of a team's pitchers and all of its hitters are grouped together to get team totals in these categories, and teams earn points based on their standing in the league. Whichever team has the most total points at the end of the season is the league champion.

S

salary cap—The maximum total amount a team can pay its players.

shutout—A baseball game in which one team fails to score.

simulation games—A game that allows you to manage your own team and make changes batter by batter. Unlike fantasy games, simulation games don't reflect the current performance of players; they are based on past performance of major-league players.

Small World Baseball—A league that combines traditional fantasy play with a stock market-like twist. Your team accumulates points for its play on the field. In addition, Small World sets a player's value based on how many teams in all of its leagues have that player on their roster. You have a set budget with which to work, but player values change each day. The idea is to "buy" players at a low value and "sell" them when their value is high.

Southeastern Conference—The SEC is one of the top conferences in college baseball in the United States. Among its powerhouse teams are Louisiana State, Alabama, and Arkansas.

spring training—Preseason games played by major-league teams in Arizona or Florida. Spring training serves as a warm-up for the regular season and an opportunity for players to show themselves worthy to make the team.

standings—A list of teams ranked in order by their number of wins and losses.

statistics—A collection of quantitative data.

stats service—In fantasy baseball leagues, where keeping up with statistics can be a chore, stats services—usually for a fee—will give you their software so you can download statistics from their Web page whenever you want them.

T

trajectory—The path a baseball takes whether it is hit or thrown.

Twentieth Century Baseball Association—A group of APBA-based leagues that replay major-league seasons from a variety of eras.

U

umpire—The official who rules on plays in baseball.

USA Baseball—The organization that governs national teams at levels ranging from 16-and-under to the Olympic teams.

W

winter ball—A form of minor league baseball, winter ball offers players a chance to improve in the offseason.

INDEX

NUMBERS

123 Baseball Web site, 25
2000 Olympic Games, 118

A

A League of Their Own, 34
AAGPBL (All-American Girls
  Professional Baseball League),
  34-35
AAU (Amateur Athletic Union),
  110, 221
ABUA (Amateur Baseball
  Umpires Association), 15
Accubat, 25, 221
Adobe Acrobat Reader, 12
African American players, 33-34
Alibris.com Web site, 152
All-American Girls Professional
  Baseball League (AAGPBL),
  34-35
All-American Professional
  Baseball League, 221
Amateur Athletic Union (AAU),
  110, 221
amateur baseball, 103
  Amateur Athletic Union, 110
  high school, 107-108
  Little League Baseball,
    108-110
  local level, 104
    American Legion
      baseball, 104
    Babe Ruth Baseball,
      105
    high school, 107-108
  Olympics, 117

PONY League baseball, 108
  related Web sites, 216
Amateur Baseball Umpires
  Association (ABUA), 15
Amazon.com Web site, 170-172
America's Pastime's Baseball
  Cards Web sites, 162
American Legion baseball, 104,
  221
  forming a league, 104
  history, 105
  Lower Montco League, 106
  rules, 11
  Web site, 12, 104
American Mold Web site, 25
Anaheim Angels Web site, 50
Angela Fremont's Web site, 175
Angell, Roger, 153
AOL
  Channels, 187
  chat rooms, 72, 193-194
  fantasy baseball, 194
  setting shortcuts, 192
  Sports Channel, 188
    Baseball forum, 190
    Baseball screen, 189
    baseball stats, 192
    checking scores, 191
  subscribers, 187
  Team Clubs link, 194
APBA Baseball, 149
Arizona Diamondbacks Web site,
  50
Arizona Fall League, 91-92, 221
artwork (baseball), 175
Atlanta Braves Web site, 50
auctions, 167
audio clips, MLB Web site, 30

J

Jackson, Shoeless Joe, 29
James, Bill, 61, 152
Japanese baseball, 113-114
    Fukuoka Daiei Hawks, 116
    players, 114-115
        American, 115
        Hideo Nomo, 115
        Masanori Murakami,
        114
    Web site, 115
Jay Buckley's Baseball Tours, 178-179
joining
    AOL, 187
    chat rooms, 73
    coaches associations, 22
    fantasy leagues, 128-132
    newsgroups, 77
    online gaming leagues, 154

K - L

Kansas City Royals Web site, 51
Kim, Wendell, 20

Latin American baseball, 113
leagues
    APBA Baseball, 149
    International, 89
    North American Strat-O-
    Matic Baseball League, 149
    Northern, 90
    online gaming, 153-154
Library of Congress' online
    archive of baseball cards Web
    site, 162
list drafts, 131, 223
listserv. *See* mailing lists
Little League Baseball, 108, 223
    parents' code of conduct, 14
    rules, 13-14
    Web site, 13, 109
    World Series, 13, 109-110
live baseball coverage online, 45
live drafts, 131, 223

local media outlets, 54
Los Angeles Dodgers Web site, 51
Lower Montco League of
    American Legion baseball Web
    site, 106

M

magazines
    Baseball America, 85-86
    Baseball Weekly, 43
magic number, 224
mailing lists, 78, 224
    Team Clubs link (AOL), 194
Major League Baseball Statistics
    Web site, 66
Major League Baseball. *See* MLB
memorabilia, 159, 224
    bobbing-head dolls, 165
    online auctions, 167
    related Web sites, 218
    uniforms/equipment, 163
message boards, Board Talk
    (AOL), 193
messages, posting to bulletin
    boards, 74
Metrodome, 178
Miami Hurricanes, 98
Mills, Dick, 18
Mills, Ryan, 19
Milwaukee Brewers Web site, 51
Minnesota Twins
    WCCO 4000, 55
    Web site, 51
minor league baseball, 83
    2000 Olympic Games, 118
    Arizona Fall League, 91-92
    ESPN.com, 85-86
    fantasy leagues, 135
    farm teams, 223
    independent leagues, 83, 90
    official team site reports, 52
    related Web sites, 215
    Web sites, 84
        Baseball America
        Online, 86-87
        league specific, 89

Northern League, 90, 224
    Web site, 91

O

Oakland Athletics Web site, 51
Oh, Sadaharu, 114
Olympic baseball, 117
    2000 Olympic games, 118
    history, 117-119
    NBC's Olympics Web site,
        118
Once More Around the Park, 153
online auctions, 167
ordering baseball strategy games
    online, 147
Outlook Express, 77

P

pennants, 224
Philadelphia Phillies Web site, 51
The Pitch That Killed, 153
pitching
    closers, 222
    Dick Mill's pitching site, 18
    injuries, Ryan Mills, 19
    Japanese pitchers, 115
Pittsburgh Pirates Web site, 51
planning baseball vacations
        museums, 182, 185
        spring training, 181-182
        Web sites, 219
        working with
            companies, 178-181
players
    American players in Japan,
        115
    biographies, 170
    Casey Stengel, 202
    closers, 222
    Cuban, 113
    fantasy baseball, 126
    injury reports, 133
    Japanese, 113-115
    Latin American, 113

Negro Leagues, 33-34
nicknames, 58, 203
prospects, 225
Ryan Mills, 19
salary information, 42
Shoeless Joe Jackson, 29
Web sites, 56-57
PONY League Baseball, 224
    Web site, 108
posting messages to bulletin
    boards, 74
private fantasy baseball leagues,
    139
prizes (fantasy/rotisserie baseball),
    131
prospects, 225
    Arizona Fall League, 91
    list of, 87
public fantasy baseball leagues,
    139

R

Rawnsley, David, 86
RBIs, 225. *See also* stats
Real Audio player, 31
Rodrigues, Tom, 175
Roth, Philip, 169
rotisserie baseball, 125-126
    commissioners, 138
    communicating with league
        members online, 142, 144
    drafts, 131-132
    joining leagues, 128, 130, 132
    joining leagues online, 129
    leagues, 225
    online resources, 132, 137
        Commissioner.com, 140
    playing online, 127
    public/private leagues, 139
    setting up online, 138
    stats
        Internet-based services,
            137
        online services, 141-142
Web sites, 134

Tell Us What You Think!

As the reader of this book, *you* are our most important critic and commentator. We value your opinion and want to know what we're doing right, what we could do better, what areas you'd like to see us publish in, and any other words of wisdom you're willing to pass our way.

I welcome your comments. You can email or write me directly to let me know what you did or didn't like about this book—as well as what we can do to make our books stronger.

Please note that I cannot help you with technical problems related to the topic of this book, and that due to the high volume of mail I receive, I might not be able to reply to every message.

When you write, please be sure to include this book's title and author as well as your name and phone or fax number. I will carefully review your comments and share them with the author and editors who worked on the book.

Email: *internet_sams@mcp.com*

Mail: Mark Taber
            Associate Publisher
            Sams Publishing
            201 West 103rd Street
            Indianapolis, IN 46290 USA

SAMS
Teach Yourself
Today

Sams Teach Yourself e-Travel Today

Planning Vacations, Finding Bargains, and Booking Reservations Online

Mark Orwoll
ISBN: 0-672-31822-9
$17.99 US/$26.95 CAN